LEGACY *of the* LANDSCAPE

LEGACY

of the LANDSCAPE

AN ILLUSTRATED GUIDE TO HAWAIIAN ARCHAEOLOGICAL SITES

Patrick Vinton Kirch

Photographs by
Thérèse I. Babineau

University of Hawai`i Press
Honolulu

For Barbara Ver Kirch
and Harold William Kirch

© 1996 University of Hawai'i Press
All rights reserved

Designed by Brian Ellis Martin
Produced by Marquand Books, Inc., Seattle
Printed in Singapore

96 97 98 99 00 01 5 4 3 2 1

Library of Congress Cataloging-in-Publication Data

Kirch, Patrick Vinton.
    Legacy of the landscape : an illustrated guide to Hawaiian
archaeological sites / Patrick Vinton Kirch : photographs by
Thérèse Babineau.
        p.   cm.
    Includes bibliographical references and index.
    ISBN 0-8248-1816-4 (hardback)
        0-8248-1739-7 (paperback)
    1. Hawaiians—Antiquities. 2. Man, Prehistoric—Hawaii.
3. Excavations (Archaeology)—Hawaii. 4. Hawaii—Antiquities. I. Babineau, Thérèse. II. Title.
GN875.H3K55   1996
996.9'1—dc20   95-41637

University of Hawai'i Press books are printed on acid-free
paper and meet the guidelines for permanence and durability
of the Council on Library Resources.

CONTENTS

PREFACE

To the average visitor, the Hawaiian Islands are famous for their salubrious climate and inviting beaches. A smaller number of visitors are attracted by the native wet and dry forests with their unique plants and fauna, and those with a natural history background realize that the Islands harbor more unique—and endangered—species than any other part of the United States. Even less well known to most, Hawai'i boasts a rich heritage of archaeological sites, the legacy of hundreds of years of occupation by Polynesian people who were the first to discover and settle the archipelago. Many of these sites are accessible to visitors and local residents alike, but authoritative guides to these ruins are sorely lacking. Archaeological information presented in standard tour guides is spotty and frequently inaccurate, and the task of seeking out descriptions of sites in scholarly volumes published for professional archaeologists will deter all but the most diligent student.

Archaeological sites have varied meanings and significance to different people; they are complexly linked to the contemporary cultural values of different sectors of our multicultural society. To the native Hawaiian people, these sites constitute geographic links with their history and cultural heritage, sacred places *(wahi pana)* within a landscape vastly transformed by two centuries of economic "development" that has more often than not ravaged the land. Edward Kanahele writes that such *wahi pana* tell him "who I am and who my extended family is. A place gives me my history, the history of my clan, and the history of my people." Yet appreciation of archaeological sites is certainly not limited to those of Hawaiian ancestry. Local residents of the islands—whatever their ethnic or cultural heritage—frequently have a strong interest in these places that have such great power to inform and educate us about the past. Likewise, many visitors to the Islands have a desire to learn and to be enriched by the archaeological heritage of Hawai'i, just as visitors to

other regions of the world have long sought out the monuments and archaeological vestiges of other great cultures. Thus, while the native Hawaiian people must always have the first say in contemporary efforts to preserve and curate the archaeological legacy of Hawai'i, no single group can ever have an exclusive claim on the past. Individual sites as property may be owned and controlled, but the past is not a piece of real estate to be bought or sold. No one "owns" the past, even though at certain times fierce social and cultural struggles may rage over control and representation of the past. Some recent events—such as the highly emotional and public controversy surrounding sites at Hālawa and Luluku in the path of the H-3 Freeway corridor on O'ahu—make it clear that the archaeological landscape can be a highly charged arena of cultural and political discourse in modern Hawai'i.

Efforts to protect and preserve archaeological sites in the Islands have a long history, resulting from the efforts of various individuals and citizens' groups, of the Territorial and later State of Hawaii government, and of the federal government (especially the National Park Service). As a result, a substantial number of sites distributed over the main islands have not only been protected from the incursions of land "development," but made accessible for visitation and appreciation by the public. Public use of these places—whether for personal enrichment, for school groups and classes, for native Hawaiian religious practices, or similar purposes—has been increasing in recent decades, as interest in Hawaiian history and culture has flourished. The present book is intended as a modest contribution toward this movement, for only when sites are culturally as well as historically interpreted will they be treated with the proper respect and appreciation they deserve.

Two principles have guided the choice of sites for inclusion in this volume. First, all sites must be accessible

Detail: "Temple du Roi dans la baie Tiritatea." (Courtesy of the Bishop Museum) (See p. 97.)

to the public, even if some restrictions apply. In most cases, the sites are situated in National or State parks, or in some cases in "historic preserves" set aside by resorts or other developments for public enjoyment. These sites generally incorporate facilities for visitors, such as parking areas and interpretive signs or exhibits. Because of their significance, however, a few sites have been included that require special permission or arrangements to visit. Where such arrangements are required, we have noted the current procedures for seeking permission and access in the text; however, the reader is cautioned that such arrangements may change in the future. Our second guiding principle was to select a range of site types so that the total ensemble would provide the reader or the visitor with a comprehensive overview of Hawaiian archaeology and prehistory. This principle was the more difficult to achieve, because by far the greatest emphasis on site preservation in Hawai'i has been on the impressive stone temple foundations known as *heiau*. But *heiau* exemplify just one aspect of ancient Hawaiian culture—that of ritual and religion—whereas we wanted to incorporate sites that would illustrate the full range of Hawaiian lifeways: agriculture, fishing, social organization, art, and so forth. While *heiau* do figure prominently in this guidebook—reflecting the long-standing interest in their preservation—the reader will also find house sites and village complexes, canoe sheds, fishponds, dryland agricultural field systems, irrigation canals, terraced cultivation complexes, fortifications, petroglyphs, stone trails, and other types

of sites. Unfortunately, it has not been possible to include every site category. For example, we were unable to find an example of a *hōlua* slide that was accessible to the public.

Most of the sites described and illustrated herein are *prehistoric*; in other words, they date to the period prior to European arrival in A.D. 1778. However, we have also included a few significant archaeological sites dating to the postcontact period, such as the Russian Fort Elizabeth on Kaua'i, and John Young's house site on Hawai'i. These historic period sites represent some of the major social and political transformations that swept through the Islands during the nineteenth century.

In some respects this book may be used as a field companion to my more comprehensive work on Hawaiian archaeology, *Feathered Gods and Fishhooks: An Introduction to Hawaiian Archaeology and Prehistory* (University of Hawai'i Press, 1985). *Feathered Gods and Fishhooks*, which discusses most of the sites covered in the present book, is a general synthesis of ancient Hawaiian lifeways and cultural developments as revealed in the archaeological record. Unlike this guidebook with its site-by-site organization, *Feathered Gods and Fishhooks* is thematically structured, and includes a comprehensive bibliography of primary sources on Hawaiian archaeology. These two books are designed to complement each other in providing an overview of Hawaiian archaeology that is scholarly yet readable.

PHOTOGRAPHER'S NOTE

All of the photographs were made with a 500 C/M Hasselblad medium-format camera. I used two Zeiss lenses, an 80 mm and a 50 mm, the latter of particular use for architectural details. A Bogen tripod came in handy for most of the shots; the camera had to be hand-held to get some of the images. I did not use any filters. A Pentax digital spot-meter was my light meter of choice. A Sekonic incident light meter was used as a backup and to cross-check exposure readings. Exposures for this project ranged from 1/500th of a second to 16 seconds.

I used Agfa film (Agfapan 25, 100, and 400), which was developed with Kodak's D-76. I printed the photographs on Oriental Seagull fiber-based paper, using grades 2 and 3, which I chose for its rich tonal range and cold tone. Kodak's Dektol was the developer. To create the fine prints, I varied the developer's dilution ratio from the standard 1:2 (one part developer to two parts water) to 1:4, and for some prints, even 1:1.

Photographing archaeological sites on the beautiful Hawaiian Islands was a collaborative effort. Without the help of my partner and husband, Patrick V. Kirch, the project would not have been actualized. We developed an effective system, combining our joint knowledge of archaeology and photography. Once on the Islands, we had to work with intense sunlight, vagaries of weather, and a tight schedule. Although photographing after 9:30 A.M. and before 4 or even 5 P.M. was not desirable, there were times when our choice was either to "go for it" or not to include the site in this book. We opted for the former.

ACKNOWLEDGMENTS

During a vacation at Kīlauea, Hawaiʻi, in December 1991, Thérèse Babineau and I visited Wahaʻula Heiau, built according to Hawaiian tradition by the voyaging Tahitian high priest Paʻao in the thirteenth century. Wahaʻula had barely been spared from Pele's wrath in the recent lava flows, and I asked Thérèse if she would take some medium-format black-and-white photos of the site. We later hiked to the wonderful petroglyph field at Puʻuloa, where Thérèse captured photographic images of some of the most intriguing glyphs. An illustrated guide to accessible Hawaiian archaeological sites—written for the intelligent and interested public—had long been a "back-burner" project about which I would muse periodically. While hiking over the lava flows to Puʻuloa, it occurred to us to combine my expertise in Hawaiian archaeology with Thérèse's photographic skills, to make the long-deferred archaeological guidebook a reality. We began to plan such a project, making a formal proposal to the University of Hawaiʻi Press the following year. With the Press' enthusiastic support, we spent the summer months of 1993 carrying out the necessary photographic fieldwork. All of the photos in this book were exposed specifically for this project, and the images reproduced here have been selected from among some 1,680 2.25-inch format negatives.

Financial assistance to underwrite a significant portion of the costs of photographic fieldwork and photo processing was provided by a grant from the Stahl Fund administered by the Archaeological Research Facility, University of California at Berkeley. Sherry Parrish, ARF administrator, helped with accounting and provided other assistance.

Many friends and acquaintances provided assistance and support during our 1993 photographic fieldwork in the Islands. On Kaua'i, David Boynton guided me to several sites and shared his extensive knowledge of the island's natural and cultural history. Kent Lightfoot was a cheerful companion in the work both on Kaua'i and at Kalaupapa, Moloka'i. Nancy McMahon, State of Hawaii archaeologist for Kaua'i, answered numerous questions about possible sites to include in our survey, and kindly supplied us with copies of Hawai'i Register of Historic Places site files.

Our stay on Moloka'i was made especially enjoyable through the gracious hospitality of Dave and Dorothe Curtis, who also loaned us their four-wheel drive vehicle. Glenn and Mahealani Davis provided the highlight of our fieldwork with a boat excursion from Hālawa to Wailau Valley; swimming ashore at Hāka'a'ano to reconnoiter archaeological sites while Glenn caught supper with his throw net was an adventure to be long remembered. Buddy Neller generously toured us around Kalaupapa, leading us through dense undergrowth to sites he had only recently discovered.

Our Lāna'i fieldwork was aided by the use of Mike Pfeffer's delightful plantation house in Lāna'i City. We also thank Mr. Saul Kaho'ohalahala for valuable information on the current state of archaeological sites on the island.

My longtime friend on Maui, Charlie Ke'au, guided us around Pihana and Haleki'i Heiau, adding to the written sources on these sites with oral traditions handed down by his grandmother. Diane Ragone of the Pacific Tropical Botanical Garden kindly granted permission for us to visit and photograph Pi'ilanihale Heiau, one of the most stunning of all Hawaiian archaeological monuments.

On Hawai'i, Leimomi Lum of the Mo'okini Luakini Foundation discussed aspects of Mo'okini Heiau, which she most lovingly curates. Laura Carter of the National Park Service gave us a personal tour of the Kaloko National Historical Park. Brian Meilleur, formerly ethnobotanist in charge of the Bishop Museum's Amy Greenwell Ethnobotanical Garden, gave us free rein to photograph the Kona Field System remains situated within the Garden.

At the University of Hawai'i Press, Executive Editor Iris Wiley enthusiastically embraced our book proposal at an early stage, and helped to expedite contracts, advances, and editorial production. Others who helped in crucial ways that they will recognize are Michael H. Kirch and Barbara Dales. *Mahalo!*

I take this opportunity especially to thank my parents, Barbara Ver Kirch and Harold William Kirch, who encouraged my early interest in Hawaiian culture and history, provided me with the opportunity to study archaeology in two of the world's finest universities, and who over the years have always lent their support. To them I dedicate this book.

Patrick Vinton Kirch
El Sobrante
March 1995

AN INTRODUCTION TO HAWAIIAN ARCHAEOLOGY

At the rear of an earthen-floor enclosure in Hōʻal Heiau, a low stone altar still receives offerings. (See p. 27.)

Detail: The isolated peninsula of Kalaupapa affords spectacular views of the windward coast of Molokaʻi, indented by Waikolu, Pelekunu, and Wailau valleys. (See p. 47.)

Peaks of great submarine volcanoes rising tens of thousands of feet from the North Pacific abyss, the Hawaiian Islands are geographic marvels. Constructed of countless lava eruptions issuing from a "hot spot" on the mid-Pacific ocean floor, each successive volcano gradually became dormant, then extinct, as it moved along a relentless path of northwestern migration driven by the earth's tectonic engine. Youthful islands such as Hawaiʻi and Maui, with their barren lava fields and rocky shores, will in time weather into older islands such as Oʻahu and Kauaʻi, with their exquisitely sculpted mountains, fertile river valleys, and coral-reef rimmed coasts.

Although the Hawaiian Archipelago is the most isolated on the planet, certain kinds of plants and animals managed to disperse and colonize these volcanic lands. From colonizing ancestral species there evolved thousands of species of trees, shrubs, herbs, birds, insects, and landsnails, most of which are endemic (found nowhere else on earth). This remote chain of islands, with its highly varied landforms and endemic plant and animal life, evolved ever so gradually over more than 40 million years. Throughout perhaps the last million years, when modern humans evolved in Africa and spread out first through Europe, Asia, and Australia, and later into the Americas, Hawaiʻi remained in total isolation. Only within the past two thousand years did *Homo sapiens* reach these island shores in sailing canoes of Polynesian origin. This event—the discovery and settlement of the Hawaiian Islands by seafaring Austronesian peoples—was to change forever the course of the archipelago's history, and to result in the rise of the most spectacular and vibrant of the Polynesian cultures.

The Polynesian Discovery of Hawaiʻi

Precisely in what year the first double-hulled voyaging canoes were hauled ashore after crossing thousands of miles of open sea is a question that will probably never be answered. Nor are we likely to ever determine the exact island that was the immediate departure point for these intrepid explorers, or on which of the Hawaiian Islands they first made landfall. Nonetheless, archaeology and its allied disciplines of historical linguistics and biological anthropology have made great strides in reconstructing in general terms the history of Polynesian settlement. The discovery and colonization of Hawai'i was, indeed, part of a remarkable saga of the human exploration and expansion into the whole of the Pacific Islands region, covering about one-third of the earth's surface.

The islands of the Pacific—known collectively as Oceania—are generally divided by anthropologists and geographers into three regions: *Melanesia*, including the vast tropical island of New Guinea and the extensive archipelagoes of the Solomons, Vanuatu, New Caledonia, and Fiji: *Micronesia*, lying north of the equator and including the many atolls of the Caroline and Marshall Islands, along with various volcanic and upraised coral islands; and *Polynesia*, the great triangular region whose apexes are marked by New Zealand, Easter Island, and Hawai'i. These three geographic regions incorporate thousands of islands and a great diversity of peoples and cultures. Despite such diversity, the majority of these peoples share common features of biology, language, and culture that provide important clues to the complex history of human migrations into this island realm.

All of the indigenous peoples within Oceania speak languages classified as either Papuan or Austronesian. The Papuan languages, however, are geographically confined to Melanesia, and in particular are concentrated on New Guinea and to a limited extent on nearby islands such as New Britain. The ancestors of the Papuan language speakers probably migrated into the New Guinea area during the late Pleistocene era, forty thousand or more years ago. In contrast, the Austronesian languages are much more widespread, including most of the languages spoken in Melanesia outside of New Guinea, and all of the languages of Micronesia and Polynesia. Moreover, the Austronesian language family encompasses the languages spoken in Taiwan, the Philippines, and Indonesia. Through more than a century of careful comparative study, linguists have been able to determine the genetic and historical relationships between the more than one thousand Austronesian languages, and to reconstruct a "family tree" for Austronesian extending back six thousand or more years. This linguistic evidence unequivocally indicates that the original Austronesian homeland lay within Southeast Asia, quite possibly incorporating Taiwan and adjacent parts of the Asian mainland. Between perhaps 4,000 and 2,000 B.C., a major diaspora of Austronesian-speaking peoples commenced, probably linked to their skills as outrigger canoe makers and seafarers. One branch of these Austronesian-speak-

ing peoples expanded eastward through the islands of the Philippines and Moluccas, along the northern coast of New Guinea (already inhabited by Papuan-speaking peoples), and into the Bismarck Archipelago. This early branch of Austronesian, called Proto-Oceanic by the historical linguists, was eventually to give rise to the numerous languages of island Melanesia, Polynesia, and central-eastern Micronesia.

Material evidence of this movement of Austronesian-speaking peoples into the Bismarck Archipelago in the mid-second millennium B.C. has been unearthed by archaeologists at various prehistoric settlements scattered throughout these islands. Archaeologists have come to label these sites and the characteristic artifacts they contain by the term *Lapita*, deriving from the name of one of the first of these ancient settlements to be excavated, on the island of New Caledonia. Lapita sites were generally situated along coastlines or on offshore islets, and the earliest known communities (such as Talepakemalai in the Mussau Islands) were clusters of thatched houses erected on stilts or piles out over shallow tidal reef flats or lagoons. Despite a strong maritime orientation, however, the Lapita people were also horticulturalists who planted a variety of root and tuber crops on the adjacent high islands. They also made and traded an elaborately decorated earthenware pottery, in which the intricately executed designs frequently portrayed human faces along with geometric motifs.

Beginning about 1600 B.C., when the first Lapita sites appeared in western Melanesia, the Lapita culture expanded rapidly eastward into the previously uninhabited islands of Melanesia and on into the Polynesian archipelagoes of Tonga and Samoa, which were settled by 1200 B.C. By the beginning of the first millennium B.C., Lapita settlements had been established throughout the cluster of archipelagoes including Fiji, the Lau Group, Futuna, 'Uvea, Tonga, Niuatoputapu, and Samoa. It was in this region—known collectively to anthropologists as Western Polynesia—that the distinctive characteristics of *Polynesian* language and culture developed over the next few centuries. Thus all Polynesian cultures, including Hawaiian, trace their origins back to the eastern branch of the Lapita culture.

During the first millennium B.C., continued changes in language and culture in the Western Polynesian homeland led to the emergence of a distinctive ancestral Polynesian culture. Continued interisland voyaging for trade and exchange helped to encourage the refinement of open-sea voyaging technology and skills, although these people also continued to depend to a large extent upon their horticultural base for subsistence. One curious development was a gradual decline in the quality and frequency of pottery manufacture, and the ceramic art eventually was abandoned by Polynesians early in the first millennium A.D. Consequently, pottery sherds are absent from Polynesian archaeological sites dating after this period, including those in Hawai'i.

The final phase in the exploration of the Polynesian islands probably began late in the first millennium B.C., with eastward voyages leading to the discovery of the southern Cook Islands, the Society Islands, and the Marquesas. Established settlements on these islands began soon thereafter, the date being a matter of current debate among archaeologists. It was from these central Polynesian archipelagoes that the final diaspora took place to the most remote islands on earth: Easter Island, New Zealand, and Hawai'i. Exactly when the Hawaiian group was first discovered remains a matter of debate, although most scholars would agree that this event occurred no later than about A.D. 600, and some would place the date several centuries earlier. The reason we cannot be more precise is that finding the first colonization site is akin to the old "needle in the haystack" problem. Likewise, determining the immediate source island for the first voyaging canoes is difficult to pinpoint, although one of the Marquesan islands is the most likely candidate.

Although it is unlikely that the *first* settlement site in the Hawaiian Islands will ever be located or excavated (indeed, it is probable that many early sites have been destroyed through years of intensive agricultural, residential, and commercial development in prime areas of the islands), archaeologists have succeeded in finding several sites dating to the early period of Polynesian settlement of the islands. One such early hamlet was situated at the mouth of the Hālawa Valley on Moloka'i Island (Site 17), while another early fishing settlement was located at South Point (Ka Lae), on Hawai'i Island (Site 47). These and other sites have yielded fishhooks, adzes, ornaments, and other artifacts with stylistic features linking them to sites of similar age in the Marquesas and Society Islands of central Polynesia. These early Hawaiian settlements also provided archaeological evidence that the Polynesian colonizers brought with them both the crop plants and

domestic animals (dogs, pigs, and chickens) necessary to establish their horticultural economy in these new lands.

Even though the distances between Hawai'i and the islands of central Polynesia (such as Tahiti and the Marquesas) are formidable, it appears that the Polynesian seafarers made a number of return voyages between these archipelagoes. Certainly Hawaiian oral traditions speak extensively and eloquently of great navigator priests and chiefs, such as Pā'ao, or Moikeha and his son Kila, who guided their double-hulled canoes safely between "Kahiki" (Tahiti) and the Hawaiian Islands. Recent experimental voyages using the reconstructed Polynesian voyaging canoe *Hōkūle'a* have shown that such inter-archipelago sailing—while requiring considerable skill and knowledge is not as daunting as once thought by some armchair scholars.[1] Nonetheless, at some point in Hawaiian history such long-distance voyaging did cease, and became only a memory encoded in myth and tradition. Just when the voyages between Hawai'i and the central Polynesian homeland ceased is not certain, although it may have been around the thirteenth century A.D. From that time until A.D. 1778, when H.M.S. *Resolution* and *Discovery* under the command of Captain James Cook pierced the horizon beyond Kaua'i, Hawai'i became an isolated world unto itself.

The Development of Hawaiian Society

While sharing features of language and culture in common with other Polynesian groups, the Hawaiian society that greeted Cook's ships in A.D. 1778 was in many respects unique and distinctive. In part, this was a result of the archipelago's isolation from other Polynesian island societies, each of which had evolved along its own individual path of cultural change. Understanding how Hawaiian culture and society developed and changed over the many centuries following initial discovery and settlement is one of archaeology's primary goals. Describing the complex processes of cultural change is a difficult task, and the following is only a brief, skeletal outline of some of the main developments.[2] In order to describe cultural change over time, archaeologists and prehistorians frequently make use of what is called a culture-historical framework or *periodization* scheme. Although cultural

1. An authoritative yet highly readable account of these experimental voyages and their anthropological significance is provided by Ben Finney, 1994, *Voyage of Rediscovery: A Cultural Odyssey Through Polynesia*, Berkeley: University of California Press.

2. More detailed discussions of prehistoric cultural changes in Hawai'i are to be found in P. V. Kirch, 1985, *Feathered Gods and Fishhooks: An Introduction to Hawaiian Archaeology and Prehistory*, Honolulu: University of Hawai'i Press; and P. V. Kirch, 1990, "The Evolution of Socio-Political Complexity in Prehistoric Hawaii: An Assessment of the Archaeological Evidence," *Journal of World Prehistory* 4:311–345.

change is in reality continuous, the entire sequence of Hawaiian prehistory is subdivided for convenience into a series of *periods*, just as European history is often subdivided into such temporal categories as the Middle Ages, the Renaissance, the Industrial Revolution, and so forth. For Hawai'i, the periods that have been defined and are used by most archaeologists are: the Colonization Period (A.D. 300–600); the Developmental Period (A.D. 600–1100); the Expansion Period (A.D. 1100–1650); and the Proto-Historic Period (A.D. 1650–1795).

The Colonization Period remains the least well documented or understood, because this phase of initial settlement and discovery is evidenced by only a handful of sites, such as those at South Point (Hawai'i) and at Waimānalo (O'ahu). Indeed, archaeologists actively debate the timing of initial Polynesian settlement of the islands, with estimates falling between about A.D. 300 or earlier and A.D. 750, although a few scholars would champion dates both earlier and later than this range. As mentioned above, the source of the first voyagers to the islands was certainly from one of the central Polynesian archipelagoes, most likely the Marquesas or the Society Islands.

Despite these ambiguities regarding the precise timing and immediate source of the Polynesian discoverers of Hawai'i, archaeologists have gleaned some understanding about this early time period. Given that Colonization Period sites are extremely rare, we can infer that the initial population was quite small, perhaps limited to a few canoe loads of people, numbering at most a hundred or so. These intrepid explorers came fully equipped and supplied to establish a permanent settlement in whatever lands they hoped to find, and carried with them the essential biological basis for their survival, namely crop plants and domestic animals. The introduction of crop plants was particularly important, because the Hawaiian Islands—despite their rich endemic flora—sorely lacked food plants useful to humans. In the tradition of their Lapita ancestors, the Polynesians carried with them root crops including taro (*Colocasia esculenta*) and yams (*Dioscorea alata*), bananas (*Musa* hybrids), sugarcane (*Saccharum officinarum*), and tree crops such as breadfruit (*Artocarpus altilis*) and coconut (*Cocos nucifera*). They also brought the sweet potato (*Ipomoea batatas*), a root crop of South American origin that had been introduced prehistorically into central Polynesia. (There is some possibility that the sweet potato did not

arrive with the very first colonizers of Hawai'i, but was introduced later, during the Developmental or even early Expansion Periods, on one of the two-way voyages between Hawai'i and central Polynesia.) These and other cultigens, along with domestic pigs, dogs, and chickens, were to provide the basis for an intensive horticultural economy.

The early settlers were also skilled fishermen, a tradition they again inherited from their Lapita ancestors. The early Colonization Period sites have yielded a variety of fishhooks expertly manufactured from pearl shell and bone, and adapted to fishing in a range of inshore and deep-sea habitats. These fishhooks were made in distinctive styles quite similar to those found in early Marquesan archaeological sites, and provide critical evidence linking the first discoverers of Hawai'i with the Marquesas Islands of central Polynesia. Similarly, adzes of polished basalt stone found in these early contexts are also of forms related to early Polynesian adzes in the Marquesas and Society Islands.

The two known habitation sites of the Colonization Period are both small settlements, hamlets rather than villages in size, and were made up of clusters of pole-and-thatch houses, some of which were paved inside with fine river gravel ('ili'ili). Their inhabitants continued an ancient Polynesian tradition of burying their deceased in graves under the house floors. Until more sites of this remote time period are discovered and excavated, it will be difficult to say much regarding the social and political organization of the first Hawaiian settlers, although some

Detail: "An Offering before Captain Cook in the Sandwich Islands." (Courtesy of the Bishop Museum) (See page 104.)

things can be inferred from linguistic and comparative ethnographic evidence. This early society certainly was organized around hereditary chiefs, for the Hawaiian word for chief (*ali'i*) derives from the older Proto-Polynesian word *ariki*. However, this early society—made up of only a small population—probably would not have been as highly stratified, nor its *kapu*-system so pervasive, as in later times.

Of the Developmental Period of Hawaiian prehistory (roughly A.D. 600 to 1100) we know considerably more, thanks to the excavation of a number of habitation sites, including settlements at South Point (Site 47), in the Hālawa Valley (Site 17), and at a number of other locations throughout the Islands. The significance of this period lies in the development of *distinctively Hawaiian* cultural patterns. It was during the Developmental Period that the descendants of the first central Polynesian discoverers introduced those cultural traits and patterns that would eventually mark Hawaiian culture and society as different from other Polynesian groups.

While the population density of the archipelago during this time remained relatively low in relation to available land area, the numbers of people were increasing rapidly, as evidenced by the increased "visibility" of archaeological sites. Sites dating to the Developmental Period have been found on all of the major islands, although the preferred locations for settlements continued to be in the windward areas where there was an abundance of fresh water, fertile alluvial soils for farming, and good fishing grounds. However, toward the end of the Developmental Period sites begin to appear in the drier leeward areas, suggesting that the more desirable windward regions were already experiencing dense populations.

Developmental Period settlements continued to be small hamlet-type clusters of pole-and-thatch houses, often situated along the coast or near good fishing areas. In the Hālawa Valley on Moloka'i, one such hamlet (Site 17) was made up of round-ended houses with stone-lined hearths in the interior. This house form is similar to round-ended houses in the Society and Tuamotu Islands of central Polynesia, but this architectural style did not persist in later time periods in Hawai'i.

The development of distinctive Hawaiian cultural forms is most evident archaeologically in the record of material culture. Basalt adzes, which were the main woodworking tool of the Polynesians, were being made in new shapes and styles emphasizing a quadrangular cross-section, distinctively different from those of the Colonization Period. Likewise, the fishhook kit also displays new and distinctive Hawaiian forms. And several kinds of uniquely Hawaiian artifacts make their appearance in the Developmental Period, such as the stone bowling disc (*'ulu maika*) and the tongue-shaped neck ornament known as *lei niho palaoa* worn by chiefs and persons of rank.

The succeeding Expansion Period, from A.D. 1100 to 1650, was in many respects the most significant and critical phase for the emergence of classic Hawaiian culture and society as known from the time of Captain Cook's visit and after. Building upon the base of expanded population and distinctively new cultural patterns that had emerged over the course of the Colonization and Developmental Periods, Hawaiian society was now to undergo a highly dynamic phase of growth and intensification.

By the close of the Developmental Period, settlements had been established throughout the most desirable windward zones of the Islands, and some movement of people into the drier leeward regions had already begun. During the course of the 550-year-long Expansion Period, the archipelago-wide population would expand geometrically to several hundred thousand people. This population growth was certainly one of the most important underlying factors leading to social and cultural change. As the numbers of people multiplied, the need for additional agricultural land grew and the leeward slopes and valleys were cleared of native forest as agricultural field systems were established. By the close of the Expansion Period, vast tracts of intensively cultivated land had been opened up on the dryland slopes of Maui and Hawai'i Islands, and the traces of the garden walls are still visible today in Kohala (Site 29) and Kona (Site 43). In the already settled windward areas where stream water was abundant, the increased agricultural demand was met by developing sophisticated irrigation works for cultivating taro in flooded pondfields, in which yields are much higher than for dryland plantings. One of the finest examples of such beautifully constructed, stone-wall-faced irrigation complexes can be found in the Hālawa Valley on windward Moloka'i (Site 17). It was also during the Expansion Period that Hawaiian fishermen began to construct substantial stone-walled fishponds on the shallow reef flats, permitting them to raise prized mullet (*Mugil cephalis*) and milkfish (*Chanos chanos*) that thrived in brackish water. Examples of such fishponds—some of which are reputed in Hawaiian traditions to have been constructed by the legendary *menehune*—can also be seen on Kaua'i (Site 4), O'ahu (Site 8), and Moloka'i (Site 16).

Increased population also meant that the society as a whole was capable of greater differentiation and hierarchy. Ambitious chiefs with an eye toward aggrandizement of power and territorial acquisition could draw upon a plentiful populace for labor and warriors. The later part of the Expansion Period saw the crystallization of several characteristic aspects of Hawaiian sociopolitical organization, among them the *ahupua'a* system of land tenure and use. *Ahupua'a* consisted of pie-shaped land segments—often a river valley—that ran from the central mountains out to the sea, and thus encompassed all of the critical ecological zones of the island. Originally, in the traditional Polynesian pattern found in other island groups, these radial territories were probably held as extended family estates. During the Expansion Period, however, the Hawaiian chiefs began to assert their exclusive rights to control these lands, and a new pattern emerged in which subchiefs were assigned individual *ahupua'a* following the installation of a new paramount chief or island-wide ruler (*ali'i nui*), often following a war of succession. The commoners, or *maka'āinana*, were given rights to work their gardens and fields and build their houses on these *ahupua'a* lands in exchange for labor and tribute to the chiefs.

In consort with this new and increasingly hierarchical sociopolitical system went changes in religion and ritual practice. Hawaiian traditions relate that around the twelfth to thirteenth centuries, the practice of human sacrifice and the cult of the war god Kū were introduced to the islands by a navigator-priest from Kahiki, Pā'ao by name (see Site 50). Certainly during the Expansion Period the Hawaiian chiefs were increasingly making use of religious ideology to cement their power and position in society. Archaeological excavations at a number of stone temple foundations (see Sites 12, 21, 25, and 46) have demonstrated that major building episodes occurred during the Expansion Period, as the temple or *heiau* system began to be elaborated. By the close of the Expansion Period, *heiau* had become extensively developed and differentiated into a system of major "state" temples where the principal gods Kū and Lono were worshiped

in elaborate and sumptuous ceremonies by the ruling chiefs and their priests. The *maka'āinana*, on the other hand, worshipped primarily in smaller agricultural temples (*heiau ho'oūlu'ai*), in fishing shrines (*ko'a*), and at family shrines within the men's eating house (*mua*).

The last stage of cultural change and development prior to the arrival of Europeans, and to the integration of the islands into the World System of colonial expansion and commerce, was the Proto-Historic, from about A.D. 1650 to 1795.[3] By this time, Hawaiian society had more or less emerged into its characteristic structures of organization, including the elaborate, hierarchical system of chiefs, priests, occupational specialists, and commoner farmers and fishermen. This society was validated and held together by the equally elaborated *kapu* system of prescriptions and prohibitions; the penalties for transgressors could be severe, including death. In these and other respects, Hawaiian society had become quite differentiated from those of other Polynesian societies with which it shared a common ancestry, dating back to the Lapita voyagers. With the development of highly sophisticated and intensive agricultural and aquacultural production, an elaborate political hierarchy and land tenure system, a religious ideology and ritual practice that included war and fertility cults performed on massive stone temple platforms, and a highly stratified social structure, the Proto-Historic Hawaiian culture can be closely compared with other emergent forms of "state-level" societies elsewhere in the world (for example, the Olmec culture of Mesoamerica, the Pre-Dynastic Period of Egypt, or the Mississippian culture of North America).

A great deal is known of Hawaiian life in the Proto-Historic Period, not only through the evidence of archaeology (which is abundant because there are more sites dating to this late time period), but from the oral traditions of the Hawaiian people themselves. The Hawaiian chiefs and priests had developed a great interest in preserving their own family and political histories. Experts in the recitation of chiefly genealogies, of the political histories of the great ruling families, of the tales of the great culture heroes of the past—of the collective *mo'o'ōlelo* or history of the islands—held positions of high status and respect in Hawaiian society. After the arrival in 1820 of Protestant missionaries, who created an orthography for the Hawaiian language, a number of these highly learned Hawaiians began to set their knowledge down on paper.

3. The arrival of Captain Cook's expedition in A.D. 1778 technically marks the end of "prehistory" and the beginning of the historic (or written record) era in the islands. The terminal date of A.D. 1795 for the Proto-Historic Period, however, reflects the continuation of traditional Hawaiian patterns of political organization up until the conquest of O'ahu by the great war chief Kamehameha I. After A.D. 1795, the islands were effectively under a single government, and the influence of foreigners became increasingly prominent. The changes that swept through Hawaiian society in the late eighteenth and early nineteenth centuries are extensively described and documented in a two-volume work by P. V. Kirch and M. Sahlins, 1992, *Anahulu: The Anthropology of History in the Kingdom of Hawaii*, Chicago: University of Chicago Press.

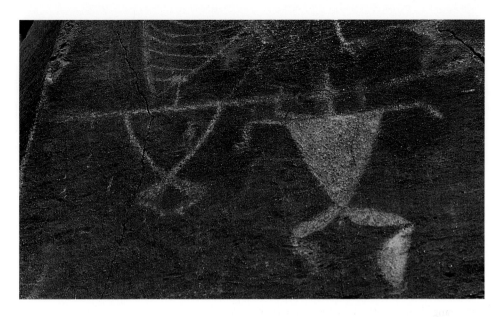

Detail: Several human figures and a "crab-claw" sail motif on the sheer cliff face at Olowalu. Modern graffiti have unfortunately marred the site. (See p. 64.)

From the writings of such men as Samuel Kamakau, John Papa ʻĪʻi, and David Malo, among others, we can relate many of the archaeological sites of the Proto-Historic Period to the events and actions of the great men and women of ancient Hawaiʻi.

Archaeology in Hawaiʻi

Despite their numerous and sophisticated developments in agriculture, the material and dramatic arts, social organization and politics—all of which rank with many of the "archaic states" or early civilizations of the Old and New Worlds—the ancient Hawaiians had not invented a writing system prior to European contact. This does not mean that the Hawaiians were unconcerned with recording their history, for their accumulated knowledge was passed on to succeeding generations through oral traditions. Fortunately, much of this ancient oral literature has come down to us today through the works of the nineteenth-century bards who set their knowledge down with pen and ink. Thus, Hawaiian traditions continue to provide an important source of information on the everyday life as well as the social and political history of Hawaiʻi in the centuries before Captain Cook broke the Islands' isolation from the Western world.

The other great source of information and potential knowledge about Hawaiian *pre*history (that is, before written documentation) must come from the material traces left in the soil and on the landscape of the islands by generations of human occupants. This material record ranges from such highly visible sites as the monumental stone temple platforms—*heiau*—that still dominate the landscape, to more subtle features, such as the low parallel ridges of ancient dryland garden fields that take a trained eye to detect. These sites, as well as the accumulations of ancient artifacts, bones, plant remains, and other detritus of human life found buried within sites, provide a richly textured and finely patterned record of Hawaiian life over hundreds of years. The discovery, study, and interpretation of such ancient sites and artifacts is the province of archaeology.

Although questions and issues of Hawaiian prehistory began to be explored soon after European contact, archaeological research per se did not begin to develop in the Islands until the close of the nineteenth century. A critical event was the founding in 1889 of the Bernice P. Bishop Museum in Honolulu. The museum's first director, William T. Brigham, began to assemble a collection of ancient stone tools and implements, publishing in 1902 an important monograph on these artifacts under the title *Stone Implements and Stone Work of the Ancient Hawaiians*. Brigham was also fascinated by the ancient religion of the Hawaiians, and he reasoned that a detailed, scientific survey of the stone temple platforms and enclosures throughout the islands could reveal much concerning Hawaiian prehistory. Brigham hired John F. G. Stokes as the Bishop Museum's curator of ethnology, and directed Stokes to survey and make accurate plans of *heiau* on Molokaʻi and Hawaiʻi Islands. Although Stokes' Hawaiʻi Island work was not published until 1991, long after his death, he nonetheless laid the groundwork for modern archaeological research in the Islands. In addition to his *heiau* surveys, Stokes conducted the first systematic sub-surface excavation in the Islands, of a fishermen's shelter cave and associated shrine on the island of Kahoʻolawe, in 1913.

During the decades between the two world wars, much basic field survey work in Hawaiian archaeology was carried out under the auspices of the Bishop Museum. Scholars including Wendell Bennett (who later became famous for his excavations in South America), J. Gilbert McAllister, Winslow Walker, and Kenneth P. Emory diligently recorded hundreds of archaeological sites throughout the Islands, focusing mostly on the monumental and often elaborately constructed *heiau*. Despite Stokes' pioneering excavations on Kahoʻolawe, virtually no excavation was undertaken during this period, primarily because it was thought that little would be gained from such tedious work. Most scholars believed that Hawaiian culture had not changed significantly prior to European arrival, and thus the existing museum collections of Hawaiian art and ethnographic artifacts, along with the oral traditions recorded by native Hawaiians themselves, provided sufficient basis for understanding the ancient culture.

These assumptions were eventually to be overthrown by Kenneth P. Emory, who in 1950 decided to thrust a trowel into the earth at Kuliʻouʻou rockshelter on the southeastern side of Oʻahu Island. Emory's excavation not only yielded a rich array of artifacts—including some types not previously represented in the Bishop Museum's collections—but provided charcoal that was tested by the newly invented technique of radiocarbon dating. Prior to the invention of radiocarbon dating by Willard C. Libby at the University of Chicago, there was no direct means of assessing the age of a prehistoric occupation site. In other parts of the world, archaeologists had developed sophisticated methods for determining chronologies based on changes in pottery types, correlating these ceramic sequences where possible with known historical events. The Hawaiians, however, did not make or use pottery, and the problem of developing a cultural sequence or chronology for the Hawaiian past had seemed intractable. Libby's revolutionary method permitted archaeologists in Hawaiʻi and other parts of the Pacific to obtain accurate estimates of age based on the radioactive decay rate of carbon 14 in organic materials (such as charcoal, wood, or bone). The sample of charcoal from Kuliʻouʻou sent to Libby by Kenneth Emory produced an estimated date of A.D. 1004 ± 180 years, considerably older than anticipated.

Inspired by these new results, Emory launched an ambitious program in Hawaiian archaeology during the 1950s, jointly supported by the Bishop Museum and the University of Hawaiʻi. In this work, which included a series of systematic excavations throughout all of the main islands, he was soon joined by his students Yosihiko Sinoto and William Bonk. By the early 1960s, Emory's research team constructed a prehistoric cultural sequence for the Hawaiian Islands based largely on radiocarbon dating, and also using changes in fishhook types, much as archaeologists elsewhere used pottery changes to construct cultural sequences. It became evident that the Hawaiian Islands were first settled some time in the early first millennium A.D., by Polynesians voyaging from one or more archipelagoes in central East Polynesia—quite likely the Marquesas Islands.

Over the past three decades, the study of Hawaiian archaeology has broadened to encompass a host of new research questions about ancient Hawaiian life, aided by the application of increasingly sophisticated techniques, methods, and interpretative theories. Rather than focusing just on the architecturally impressive *heiau*, or on coastal rockshelters and middens rich in fishhooks and other artifacts, archaeologists today are interested in the entire range of sites, and in how these features are patterned over the landscape. By analyzing the arrangement of sites, both in relation to geographic features such as streams, soils, and rainfall, and to each other, archaeologists have learned much about ancient Hawaiian social and political organization, and their economy. Rather than using radiocarbon dating merely as a tool to determine the age of a site, archaeologists are accumulating and analyzing suites of hundreds of radiocarbon dates in order to assess changes in prehistoric population growth and density. The effects of ancient Hawaiian forest clearance, agriculture, and hunting on the forests and the unique bird life and other endemic biota of the archipelago are being studied through analysis of excavated bones and plant remains, through pollen analysis of sediment cores, identification of carbonized wood in ancient hearths and oven pits, and other techniques. Archaeologists and anthropologists have come to realize that Hawaiian culture and society underwent many important changes and developments in the course of the fifteen or so centuries between initial Polynesian discovery and settlement, and the arrival of Europeans and other foreigners beginning in 1778. While understanding this history is important and fascinating in its own right, *comparison* of Hawaiian prehistory with the developmental sequences of other complex cultures and early civilizations can tell us much about general trends and processes of human societies.

The practice of archaeology in Hawaiʻi has, in recent years, come to be dominated by what is sometimes called "contract archaeology" or "cultural resource management" (CRM). Although many of the underlying research questions—as well as the basic methods and techniques—used by CRM archaeologists are identical to those in academically supported archaeological work, CRM archaeology is driven by the pressures of modern land development. Since it became the Fiftieth State in 1959, Hawai'i has undergone unprecedented economic growth, largely spurred by the international tourism industry. With the construction of hotels, resort complexes, and golf courses has come the expansion of roads, airports, harbors, water and electric lines, and other infrastructure. Most of these development projects have taken place on lands that included archaeological sites—not uncommonly, large numbers of sites—and most archaeological work being undertaken in recent years has been focused on the recording, study, salvage excavation, and, sometimes, preservation of these features.

The emphasis on CRM archaeology in Hawai'i since the early 1970s has been something of a two-edged sword. On the positive side, substantially increased funding for archaeological work has resulted in the accumulation of vast amounts of new information, ranging from basic site records, to excavated materials, to radiocarbon dates. Also on the positive side, many important sites have been saved from destruction by archaeologists who have advocated their protection and preservation. But there are negative aspects to this dominance on CRM-funded archaeology. For example, the rate of accumulation of new information has been so fast that there has often been neither sufficient time nor funds to assimilate, synthesize, and interpret the new findings. More disturbing, archaeologists have tended to become linked in the public vision with land developers. Thus archaeologists are increasingly viewed with suspicion by some people, especially native Hawaiians who are rightly concerned with their land rights and with the preservation of their cultural heritage.

The world-wide recession of the late 1980s and early 90s has brought a considerable slowdown to the pace of land development in Hawai'i, and with it a relaxation in the pace of CRM archaeology. One can only stress that perhaps this is a good time for a rethinking of the direction of archaeological work in the islands, and for a careful review and stocktaking of vast quantities of new data accumulated over the past few decades. Archaeologists working in Hawai'i can be proud of their many contributions to knowledge about the Hawaiian past, but this is no excuse for complacency. There is much to be done to assure that this knowledge be used wisely and to the benefit both of the native Hawaiian people, and of all who share a concern for and interest in the Hawaiian past.

VISITING HAWAIIAN SITES

The gently curving stone-walled arc of a prehistoric fishpond along the southern shore of Moloka'i Island, constructed from thousands of basalt and coral boulders.

The sites described and illustrated in this book were specifically selected because they are accessible to the public, although in some cases with restrictions. Most of the sites have been landscaped and modified so as to accommodate visitors, with parking areas, access trails, and markers or interpretive trails. A few of the better-maintained national and state parks are staffed with rangers or interpretive specialists, but in many locations the visitor is left unattended. Regardless of whether a site is supervised, there are a few basic rules that should govern the behavior and activities of visitors to all Hawaiian archaeological sites.

• Above all, keep in mind that these sites represent the cultural heritage of the native Hawaiian people, and as such deserve great respect. This is especially so for religious sites, such as the various *heiau* or places of worship that make up a significant number of the sites included in this volume. Prior to the abolition of the *kapu* system and ancient religion by Liholiho (King Kamehameha II) in 1819, many of these *heiau* were highly sacred places, which only the high-ranking chiefs and priests would enter. Even after the traditional rituals were no longer practiced, these sites continued to be regarded as *wahi pana*, or sacred places. They are imbued with *mana*, or spiritual power, and continue to have great significance to the native Hawaiian people. Many sites continue to be actively used for religious observances, and visitors may see recent offerings such as *kī*-leaf bundles, fruits, or lei. The visitor should behave and act in these places as one would in any other place of worship, including wearing respectful clothing (it is hardly appropriate to visit a *heiau* dressed for a picnic at the beach).

• Remember at all times that Hawaiian archaeological sites are fragile constructions. The stone walls and terrace facings that make up many sites were laid without the use of mortar, and can easily tumble or collapse. The walls enclosing *heiau* and house sites were never intended by their makers to be walked upon, and visitors should keep off such constructions at all times. Many sites have foot trails designed for visitors—please stay on these and observe all signs.

• Petroglyph or rock art sites are especially fragile and vulnerable to defacement, and many significant petroglyphs have already suffered irreversible damage. *Never apply any substance to a petroglyph*, not even chalk. Rubbings are also destructive, as these can stain and/or bruise the fragile lava. The only responsible way to record a petroglyph is to take a photograph of it. Most petroglyph sites photograph well, especially in the oblique light of early morning or late afternoon.

• Never remove anything from an archaeological site; removing stones or artifacts is not only immoral, it is illegal as well. If you should happen to observe an artifact or other culturally significant material on a site (for example, exposed by erosion), leave it in place and report your observation as soon as possible either to the ranger or staff person in charge of the site, or to the local office of the State Historic Preservation Division (most islands have State archaeologists in residence).

• Do not rearrange or modify an archaeological site in any way. This includes the regrettable practice (increasingly common) of wrapping stones in *kī*-leaves as informal offerings (what one of my native Hawaiian friends derisively calls "*pōhaku laulau*"). Contrary to popular belief, this practice is not a part of traditional Hawaiian ritual (although the use of *kī*-leaves in ritual is an ancient Polynesian practice), and only leads to the rearrangement of paving and wall stones, thus destroying the integrity of the archaeological remains.

A Note on Site Location and Access

At the time we carried out the field research for this book, all of the sites were accessible to the public, usually without any special permission or arrangements. In some cases, however, restrictions do apply, such as requesting prior permission to visit, making appointments, or signing written waivers of liability. Special conditions governing access to Sites 12, 14, 17, 18, 19, 20, 25, 32, 35, and 43 at the time of writing are noted specifically in the text for these sites. The authors assume no responsibility for future changes in access to these, or other sites, made by landholders. It is the responsibility of all visitors to check with the relevant landowners or their agents as to current conditions of access before visiting any of the sites discussed in this book. The Hawaii Visitors Bureau, the State of Hawaii Parks Division, and the State of Hawaii Historic Preservation Division can also provide information with regard to site access.

We have purposefully refrained from cluttering the text with the usual "guidebookese," especially since roads are continually being rerouted and developed in modern Hawai'i. For those who intend this book to serve as a field guide, we recommend that it be used together with a set of the excellent *Reference Maps of the Islands of Hawai'i*, compiled by James A. Bier, and published by the University of Hawai'i Press. All of the sites described herein are plotted on these maps (archaeological and historical sites are labeled in red ink). Most bookstores in the Islands carry these maps, or they may be purchased directly from the University of Hawai'i Press.

The Hawaiian place names used in this book follow Pukui, Elbert, and Mookini's authoritative *Place Names of Hawaii* (1974).

THE SITES

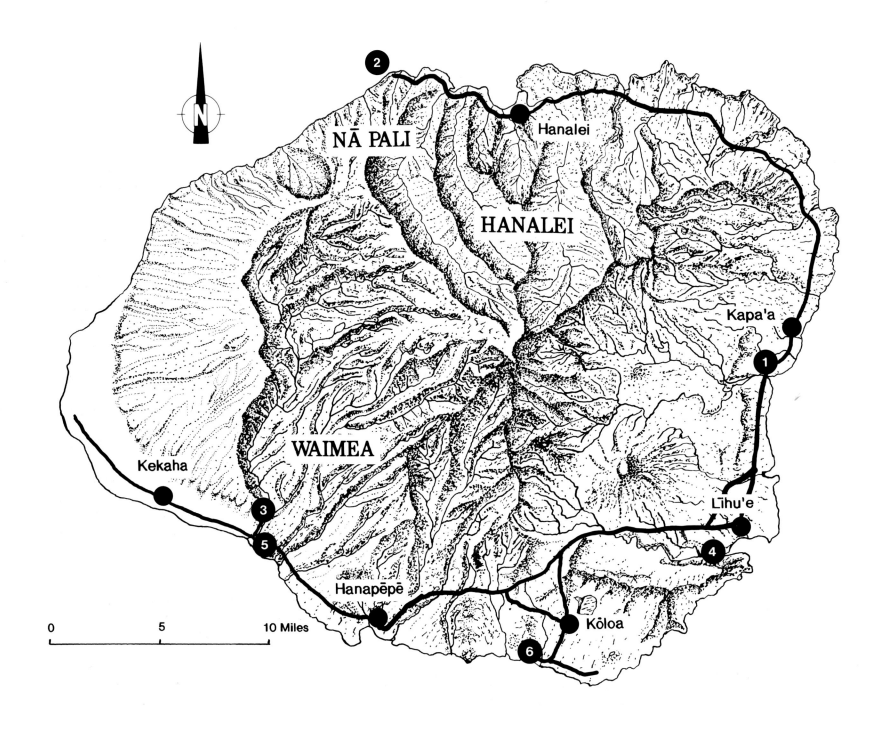

NĀ PALI

HANALEI

Hanalei

Kapa'a

WAIMEA

Kekaha

Līhu'e

Hanapēpē

Kōloa

0   5   10 Miles

KAUA'I ISLAND

Fourth largest of the Hawaiian Islands, Kaua'i lies at the western end of the archipelago, separated from O'ahu by a frequently turbulent ocean channel seventy-three miles wide. Geologically, Kaua'i is the oldest of the main islands, its volcanoes last having erupted between about four and six million years ago. After the island moved off the active volcanic "hot-spot" (today occupied by Hawai'i Island), weathering by wind and rain gradually sculpted the magnificent Nā Pali and Halele'a valleys and ridges, the deep gorge of Waimea Canyon, and deposited the fertile alluvial soils in valleys such as Wailua and Hanalei.

Traditionally, Kaua'i was divided into five political districts. On the northwest is Nā Pali (literally, "the cliffs"), whose deep valleys such as Kalalau are divided by razor-backed ridges, and are accessible only by sea or over treacherous trails. The valleys of the Halele'a District —on the northern, windward side of the island—are more readily accessible, and the abundant streamflow here made this an area rich in irrigated taro fields. The northeastern bulge comprised Ko'olau District. At the core of the island lay Puna District, with the vast and fertile Wailua and Hulē'ia river valleys. This was the great agricultural "breadbasket" of Kaua'i, and not surprisingly the island's chiefly families established their households at the mouth of the Wailua River (see Site 1). The dry, leeward side of Kaua'i comprised Kona District. It was here at the mouth of the Waimea River that Captain James Cook, commanding His Britannic Majesty's ships *Resolution* and *Discovery*, first landed on January 20, 1778. Waimea would later be the setting for an aborted attempt by the Russian–American Company to establish a fort and trading station in the Islands (see Site 5).

There are many aspects of Kaua'i archaeology and prehistoric culture that are distinctive from the rest of the Hawaiian Islands, and which have long puzzled scholars. For example, throughout the other islands the stone pounders used to make poi from taro corms were of a uniform conical shape with a knob at the top. On Kaua'i, however, two other styles of pounder were developed, one with a ringlike handle and one shaped rather like a stirrup. Archaeologists have also found on Kaua'i a kind of "block grinder" made from basalt, of uncertain function, that appears nowhere else in the archipelago. These and other distinctive aspects of the island's culture have sometimes been cited as evidence that Kaua'i was settled independently from the rest of the islands, and that the legendary *menehune* actually refers to this earlier group of people. More likely, these differences between Kaua'i and the other islands result from the considerable isolation occasioned by the distances between them, and infrequency of interisland voyages and contact. Crossing the stormy channel between O'ahu and Kaua'i by canoe can be perilous, and twice thwarted the war king Kamehameha I in his plans to subjugate the Kaua'i paramount chief, Kaumuali'i.

Kaua'i is rich in archaeological sites, although only a few have been made readily accessible to visitors, such as the six sites described on the following pages. A good introduction to the island's rich history and culture can also be obtained at the Kaua'i Museum in Lihue (4428 Rice Street).

Map of Kaua'i Island.

1. *HEIAU* COMPLEX AT WAILUA

Popularly referred to as the "Garden Isle," Kaua'i boasts extensive tracts of fertile soil and many large river valleys, all of which provided the natural resources to support a substantial population in precontact times. The greatest of these river valleys is Wailua ("two waters"), with two branches draining a vast inland region, today dominated by sugarcane plantations but formerly the agricultural core of the ancient Kaua'i chiefdom. Not surprisingly, a region so richly endowed with agricultural wealth was also the residential and religious seat of powerful chiefs and their retainers. Within a radius of about one and a half miles from the Wailua River mouth are six important temples and associated sites constructed under the aegis of these chiefs. These sites were officially designated a National Historical Landmark in 1962 (a marker commemorating this is affixed to a large boulder on the ridge seaward of Poli'ahu Heiau).

Occupying a commanding position on the narrow ridge spur dividing 'Ōpaeka'a Stream and Wailua River, ceremonies carried out at Poli'ahu Heiau would have been widely visible from the densely settled lowlands. The sheer cliffs of Mauna Kapu ("sacred mountain")— in which white-tailed tropic birds nest—loom over the site to the south. This massive temple foundation is a fine, well-preserved example of a *luakini heiau*, a class of temple built by paramount chiefs and dedicated to the god of war, Kū. Pioneering archaeologist Wendell Bennett, who mapped the site in the late 1920s, accurately described it as "a paved and walled enclosure roughly rectangular with a 30 by 70-foot notch taken out of the southeast corner." Bennett gave the *heiau* dimensions as 242 feet long by 165 feet wide. Most of the interior consists of a stone-paved court on which may be seen fallen, prismatic-shaped dikestone uprights; similar upright stones were illustrated by Captain Cook's artist, John Webber, in his famous drawing of a *heiau* at Waimea. Along the southern and western sides of the court are low, stone-faced terraces, and there are a number of pits and other architectural features in the northeast corner. Of special interest is a large rectangular boulder that was set upright against the middle of the southern enclosure wall; such stones were usually set up to represent particular deities. Below Poli'ahu Heiau on the same ridge, where

the terrain narrows, can be found a legendary "bellstone," occupying a spectacular view over the Wailua River.

Leaving Poli'ahu Heiau and proceeding towards the Wailua River mouth, one passes Holoholokū Heiau and the adjacent "birthing stones" site. (On the north side of the highway opposite these archaeological features is a charming small ethnobotanical garden). These "birthing stones" actually consist of two large natural stone outcrops, one called the *pōhaku ho'ohānau* ("stone of birth giving") and the *pōhaku piko* ("navel stone"). As with other such localities in the Hawaiian Islands (see also Kūkaniloko, Site 10), this was a place to which high-ranking chiefesses repaired to give birth to their royal offspring, and to deposit the afterbirth and umbilical cord. Nestled against the two stone outcrops is a low, rectangular stone house foundation, which presumably supported a *pili*-grass thatched house in which the actual

A large upright boulder, incorporated into the southern facing of Poli'ahu Heiau and surrounded by plantings of kī, probably represented one of the deities worshipped at this temple.

The sheer cliff face of Mauna Kapu stands sentinel across the Wailua River from Poli'ahu Heiau. A rectangular foundation for one of the temple houses is visible on the temple's court.

The seaward terrace retaining wall at Hikinaakalā Heiau incorporates a large basalt boulder with adz-grinding depressions.

The inland facing wall of Kukui Heiau, partially covered in *naupaka* and *kī* plants.

birth took place, the chiefess being surrounded and assisted by her retinue. Just seaward of the birthing stones is Holoholokū Heiau, a stone-walled enclosure built up against a low ridge with several terraces. Piercing the southern wall of the temple enclosure is a unique low "doorway." By some accounts, Holoholokū was not actually a temple at all, but a chiefly residence site.

The other sites comprising the Wailua Historical District are concentrated around the shores of Wailua Bay. On the southern shore of the Wailua River mouth lies Hikinaakalā Heiau ("rising of the sun"), also designated by some authorities as a place of refuge (*pu'uhonua*) known as Hauola. Set among coconut palms and *Pandanus* trees, Hikinaakalā was robbed of many of its stones in the past century, so that only the larger boulders originally forming the wall bases remain intact. Nonetheless, one can readily make out the three distinct paved divisions that formed this structure. Firmly set into the best preserved of these walls—an outer terrace retaining wall facing the river mouth—is a large basalt grindstone with several smooth, polished facets produced by sharpening the bevels of stone adzes. That this grindstone was taken out of secular use and incorporated into the walls of a *heiau* suggests that it may have been imbued with great *mana* or spiritual power. At low tide, the faint outlines

of petroglyphs can be discerned on a group of boulders lying in the Wailua River mouth not far from Hikinaakalā Heiau.

On the inland side of Highway 56 from Hikinaakalā Heiau is Mana Heiau, a massive rectangular walled *luakini heiau* measuring 395 feet long, making it one of the largest architectural sites on Kaua'i. At the present time, the site is not readily accessible to the public, although it is owned by the State of Hawaii, and there are plans to preserve and interpret the structure in the future.

On the northern shore of Wailua Bay, on Alakukui Point, is yet another temple: Kukui Heiau. (To visit this site, which has been donated to the State of Hawaii by the developers of the nearby condominium, follow the public access right-of-way between Lae Nani Condos and the Kauai Sands.) The site was probably modified after the overthrow of the old religion in 1819, and today is heavily landscaped. However, several impressive facing walls are visible, and the temple foundation boasts a spectacular perspective on Wailua Bay.

References: Bennett (1931:125–128); Fowke (1922:192–193).

Hikinaakalā Heiau sits on a sandy ridge at the mouth of the Wailua River.

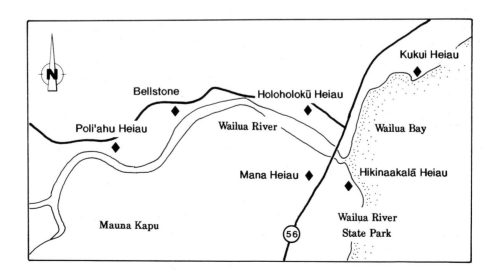

Map of the Wailua River area (Site 1).

2. KE-AHU-A-LAKA HĀLAU HULA AND KA-ULU-A-PAʻOA HEIAU AT HĀʻENA

The narrow highway that winds along the beautiful northern coast of Haleleʻa District ends at Kēʻē Bay, Hāʻena (the bay and adjacent sand dunes are part of a State park). Here at the foot of towering cliffs begins the Nā Pali trail, leading to Kalalau and other remote valleys of Kauaʻi. Situated on the steep slopes between the rocky shore of Kēʻē Bay and the vertical *pali* face are several archaeological sites that have legendary associations with the volcano goddess Pele, her younger sister Hiʻiaka, and the high chief Lohiʻau. Pele and Hiʻiaka are the protagonists in an epic myth cycle of romance, adventure, intrigue, and death that spans the island chain, recorded and published by the missionary descendant Nathaniel B. Emerson in 1915.

The dance, or hula, of ancient Hawaiʻi was typically performed in long, open-ended buildings or sheds called *hālau hula*. (The term *hālau hula* has been extended today to mean a group or society of hula dancers together with their *kumu hula*, or hula master.) Perhaps the most famous of these *hālau* formerly stood on a large, low stone platform at Kēʻē, Hāʻena. The *hālau* platform bears the formal name Ke-ahu-a-Laka, "altar of Laka," the patron goddess of dance. According to the Pele–Hiʻiaka myth, it was to this *hālau* that the spirit-body of Pele traveled, and there that the handsome chief Lohiʻau fell in love with her.

The site is readily approached by following the coastal path a few hundred feet from the road's end, past a well-maintained garden. The path turns uphill, and opens onto the massive stone platform complex of Ka-ulu-a-Pāʻoa Heiau. The *heiau* platform is surmounted by low terraces and facings, with a number of pits and depressions. The steep, grassy slope above the *heiau* is irregularly terraced. Climbing past these terraces one reaches the *hālau hula*, which consists of a leveled, earthen terrace set against the vertical cliff, retained by a well-constructed stone wall two to three feet high. Originally this terrace would have supported the thatched *hālau* structure, but today the open-air setting is regularly used by hula groups who come to dance and pay their respects to Laka.

Also at Kēʻē is the house terrace of Lohiʻau, a high stone-faced platform situated at the foot of the cliffs just above the parking area, where the Nā Pali trail begins.

References: Bennett (1931:136–138); Emerson (1915); Emory (1928); Kelly (1984).

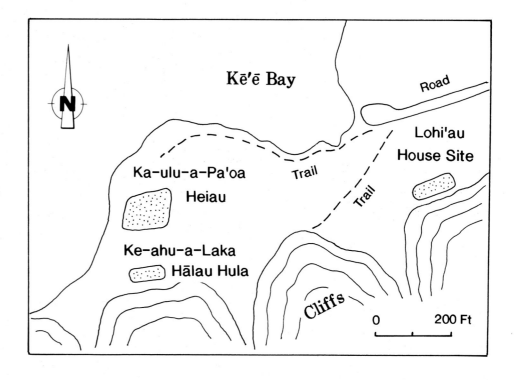

Map of Site 2 at Kēʻē.

The stone-faced terrace of Ke-ahu-a-Laka Hālau Hula lies beneath towering cliffs at Hāʻena.

3. 'AUWAI AT WAIMEA (THE "MENEHUNE DITCH")

Wherever flowing streams and rich alluvial lands were present, Hawaiians developed sophisticated irrigated agricultural field complexes for cultivating *kalo* (taro, *Colocasia esculenta*), the root crop that when mashed between a stone pounder and a wooden board, and mixed with water, makes poi. Stream water, diverted by means of stone dams, flowed through stone-lined irrigation canals (*'auwai*) to sets of rectangular pondfields. Some of these irrigation canals were more than half a mile long, carefully constructed so as to maintain a constant grade. Where the Waimea Valley begins to narrow at the foot of a prominent cliff lies a remnant portion of what archaeologist Wendell C. Bennett called "the acme of stone-faced ditches," the so-called Menehune Ditch (Kīkīaola).

While the ancient Hawaiians manufactured a diversity of tools and implements out of stone—adzes, bowls, poi pounders, *'ulu maika*, and net sinkers, for example—stone working in architectural construction is exceedingly rare. The Menehune Ditch is the finest example of such rare stone dressing in the Hawaiian Islands. Today the site consists of about 120 carefully cut-and-dressed stones,

closely fitted along a distance of some 200 feet, and forming the outer face of the irrigation canal. This canal, which still carries water to taro fields at the mouth of Waimea Valley, runs immediately adjacent to the narrow road winding between the cliff and Waimea River. A bronze plaque erected by the Territory of Hawaii in 1925 commemorates the site.

The name "Menehune Ditch" derives from a legend describing the construction of the irrigation canal by a group of *menehune* who lived near Pu'ukapele in the uplands of Waimea. Famous for their superhuman feats of construction, the *menehune* quarried and fitted the stones in a single night. The hum of their voices was sufficiently loud to be heard on O'ahu, as encoded in the proverbial saying: "*Wawa ka menehune i Pu'ukapele ma Kaua'i, puoho ka manu o ka loko o Kawainui ma O'ahu,*" which translates, "The shouts of the *menehune* on Pu'ukapele on Kaua'i startled the birds of Kawainui Pond on O'ahu" (Pukui 1983:320).

References: Bennett (1931:22–23, 105–107); Kirch (1985:104).

The finely cut and fitted basalt slabs that line the Menehune Ditch are not matched elsewhere in the islands. The slabs were prepared without the use of metal tools.

4. MENEHUNE FISHPOND

The Menehune Fishpond was constructed in a natural meander of the Hulē'ia River.

Most Hawaiian fishponds were constructed out into the ocean on sandy reef flats, as along the southern Moloka'i coastline (see Site 16). Occasionally, however, Hawaiian pond architects would make use of other suitable natural environments, such as with the famed Menehune Fishpond. (Although the pond is most widely known as the Menehune Fishpond, a reference to its having been created by the legendary *menehune*, it is also variously known as Alekoko Pond, or Niamalu Pond.) The pond makes use of a large bend in the Hulē'ia River, which flows into Nāwiliwili Bay. A stone-faced, earth-filled wall more than 900 yards long cut off this river bend, isolating the pond and permitting mullet (*Mugil cephalis*) and other brackish-water fish to be husbanded within its waters. Local lore attributes the pond's construction to the *menehune*, who are said to have completed the construction within a single night (see also Site 3). The site has never been archaeologically excavated or dated, and its actual date of construction remains unknown. The fishpond can be readily viewed from a lookout on the south side of Puhi Road.

References: Bennett (1931:124); Fowke (1922:192).

5. RUSSIAN FORT ELIZABETH

Thwarted in his plans to conquer Kaua'i Island by force, Kamehameha I in 1810 reached an accommodation with Kaumuali'i, paramount chief of the island, in which the latter would retain his sovereignty until death. Not fully satisfied with this turn of affairs, however, Kaumuali'i saw an opportunity to throw off Kamehameha's yoke when—in 1815—the Russian American Company's ship *Bering* was wrecked at Waimea Bay. (It was also at Waimea that Captain James Cook made his first landfall in the Hawaiian Islands, on January 20, 1778.) When the Russians dispatched Georg Scheffer to salvage the *Bering*'s cargo in 1816, Kaumuali'i signed a secret treaty with Scheffer in which the two parties would conspire to invade and conquer Kamehameha's domain. As the first phase in this plan, Kaumuali'i directed his forces to begin construction of a large stone-walled fort just inland of the chiefly compound, on a promontory overlooking the mouth of the Waimea River.

Fort Elizabeth—named in honor of the consort to Russian Emperor Alexander I—is a fascinating mix of European design and indigenous Hawaiian materials. The plan is roughly star shaped, with provisions for gun emplacements typical of European fortress design in the early nineteenth century. The walls were constructed under the direction of Kaumuali'i using typical Hawaiian dry-laid masonry techniques. Flights of stairs run up the inside facings of the star-pointed walls, providing access to the gun batteries. A number of stone foundations within the fort's walls that are clearly visible today supported a magazine and armory, officer's quarters, barracks, guardroom, and flagstaff. The magazine incorporated a rectangular subterranean pit lined with plaster made from burned coral, fragments of which can still be seen. A contemporary account from 1864 describes this magazine, which was roofed with heavy, sod-covered *lehua* wood beams, as "perfectly bomb-proof." The Russians also established a trading post immediately outside the main gates.

Russian occupation of Fort Elizabeth did not last long, as Scheffer's plans were vetoed by the Russian American Company directors. The Russians withdrew in 1817, but the fort continued to house a garrison of Hawaiian soldiers until about 1864. The first Protestant missionaries to arrive on Kaua'i in April of 1821, the

Rev. Samuel Whitney and his family, were also given land for their houses immediately adjacent to the fort's walls along the Waimea River bank. Fort Elizabeth has truly witnessed some of the most significant events of Hawaiian history.

The site is presently maintained as a historical park by the State of Hawaii. Archaeological survey and excavations at Fort Elizabeth were conducted by a Bishop Museum team in 1972, who found such historical artifacts as musket and cannonballs, gun flints, ramrod pipes, and a French "Phoenix" military uniform button bearing the inscription "*Je Renais de mes Cendres*." Such buttons became a Pacific trade item following the defeat of Napoleon's army at Waterloo. A renewed archaeological study of the fort by the University of California at Berkeley commenced in 1993; among other finds, the Berkeley team discovered a subterranean tunnel leading into the fort from the river side.

References: McCoy (1972); Kirch (1985:314–316, figs. 243, 244); Pierce (1965).

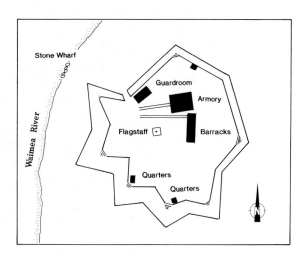

Plan of the Russian Fort Elizabeth (Site 5).

Stone steps inside Russian Fort Elizabeth lead to one of the cannon emplacements overlooking the mouth of the Waimea River.

The star-shaped defensive walls of Russian Fort Elizabeth were constructed by Hawaiian workers following a European design.

6. HŌʻAI HEIAU AND RESIDENCE (POʻIPŪ)

About two miles west of Poʻipū, and west of Waikomo Stream, lies Hōʻai Bay, the birthplace and residence of Prince Jonah Kūhiō Kalanianaole. Prince Kūhiō, who was born in 1871 of Kauaʻi *aliʻi* blood, had become the *hānai* or adopted son of Queen Kapiolani and was later named heir to the Hawaiian throne by Queen Liliʻuokalani. After the overthrow of the monarchy and the annexation of the islands as a United States Territory, Kūhiō became the Territorial delegate to Congress. Among other accomplishments, Prince Kūhiō was largely responsible for the creation of the Hawaiian Homestead Lands. Hōʻai Park, commemorating Prince Kūhiō (with its imposing monument and bust of the Prince), also contains the stone foundations of Hōʻai Heiau, a large house, fishing shrine,

and a small stone-walled fishpond. The *heiau* is unusual in plan and architecture, consisting of five raised stone platforms and earth-floored terraces adjoining a large stone-walled enclosure. At the rear or inland end of the large enclosure is a well-constructed, low stone altar. The small fishpond, located on the seaward side of the park, has been reduced in size by the road that now runs over the seawall. Near the pond are the ruins of a small *koʻa*, or fishing shrine, containing branch-coral offerings. In all, the various structures situated within Hōʻai Park provide a fine example of an *aliʻi* residential site.

Reference: Bennett (1931:117).

At the rear of an earthen-
floor enclosure in Hōʻai
Heiau, a low stone altar
still receives offerings.

A small *koa*-wood bowl
containing coral and marine
shell offerings was left by an
unknown supplicant on the
stone-slab altar of Hōʻai
Heiau.

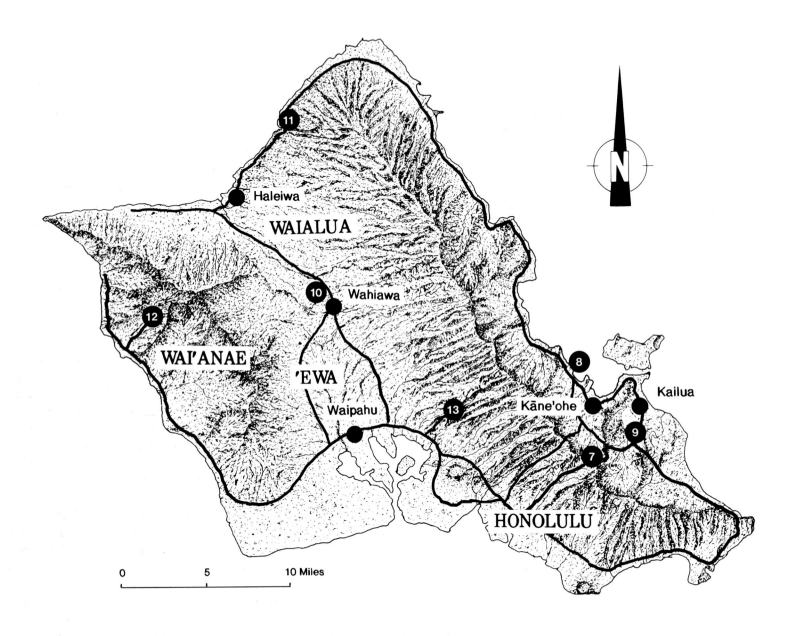

WAIALUA

Haleiwa

WAI'ANAE

'EWA

Wahiawa

Waipahu

Kāne'ohe

Kailua

HONOLULU

N

0   5   10 Miles

O'AHU ISLAND

O'ahu, slightly larger in size than Kaua'i and thus the third largest of the main islands, was formed by two coalescing volcanic mountains that last erupted between about two and three million years ago. The Ko'olau Range, the eastern spine of the island, separates the leeward Honolulu and 'Ewa regions from the windward coast. The shorter but higher Wai'anae Range creates a rain shadow that leaves the Wai'anae coast rather arid (the summit at Ka'ala reaches 4,020 feet in elevation). The saddle between the Ko'olau and Wai'anae Ranges— a plateau between 800 and 1,000 feet in elevation—today is covered largely in pineapple plantations, but it was formerly the setting for one of the most sacred locations in the archipelago, the birthing stones of Kūkaniloko (Site 10).

O'ahu was traditionally divided into six districts. The long and spectacularly beautiful windward coast was taken up by Ko'olauloa and Ko'olaupoko Districts, which met at Kualoa on the northwestern end of Kāne'ohe Bay. One of the oldest known settlements in the archipelago, excavated in the 1960s, lies behind Waimānalo Beach in Ko'olaupoko. These two districts were rich in irrigated taro lands and in fishponds. Kona District on the leeward side is somewhat drier, but abundant water from Pālolo, Mānoa, and Nu'uanu Streams nonetheless permitted the development of a vast irrigation complex and fishponds on the plain now covered by Honolulu and Waikīkī. 'Ewa District encompassed the brackish waters of Pearl Harbor, also a land rich in fishponds. Arid Wai'anae District, with its deep amphitheater-shaped valleys of Lualualei and Wai'anae, was famed for its deep-sea fishing grounds offshore; agriculture in this district was primarily of the dryland type. Finally, the lands of Waialua District on the northwestern coast, intermediate in climate, were suitable to a mix of dryland farming and irrigation.

Although O'ahu supported a large population in prehistory, the island's political and cultural dominance developed largely during the nineteenth and twentieth centuries. After conquering O'ahu in 1795, and reoccupying it in 1804, the Hawai'i Island war chief Kamehameha I established his headquarters at Honolulu. Kamehameha shrewdly recognized that control of European trade was a key to maintaining power, and the deep and protected harbor at the mouth of the Nu'uanu Stream afforded the best location to effect his strategy. Although Kamehameha I retired to his ancestral estate at Kamakahonu in Kona, Hawai'i (see Site 39) in 1812, and while for a brief time Lahaina on Maui became the capital seat of the new Kingdom, the attractions of Honolulu won out in the end.

The large population that has resided on O'ahu in the past two centuries, and the extensive commercial, agricultural, and residential developments they have engendered, have taken a devastating toll on the island's archaeological sites. When the State of Hawaii Historic Preservation Office archaeologists undertook a statewide inventory of sites in the 1970s, they found that a large number of the sites recorded in earlier decades no longer existed. Of course, many areas that are prime lands for modern development—such as the world-famous Waikīkī —were also favored dwelling areas for the ancient Hawaiian people.

A few important sites on O'ahu have been preserved and made accessible to the public. These include the massive *luakini* or war temples of Ulupō (Site 9) and Pu'uomahuka (Site 11), and the expertly restored Kāne'ākī Heiau in Mākaha Valley (Site 12). The impressive fishpond at He'eia (Site 8) and the fortifications at Nu'uanu Pali (Site 7) cannot be visited directly, but can be readily viewed from adjacent parks. Also located in Honolulu is the century-old Bernice P. Bishop Museum, whose staff has for decades been the leading force in archaeological research in the Hawaiian Islands. In addition to the Museum's public galleries, its Library and Archives provide invaluable resources for those who wish to delve more deeply into Hawaiian culture and prehistory.

Map of O'ahu Island.

7. FORTIFICATION AT NUʻUANU PALI

During the Expansion and Proto-Historic Periods, warfare between competing chiefdoms became increasingly common; such wars were often fought for control of productive agricultural lands. The Hawaiians did not build large fortresses, although they did modify natural defensive positions such as ridge tops for use as strongholds during a conflict. The most readily visible of such artificially modified ridges is at Nuʻuanu Pali, the gap or pass used as an ancient trail between the Kona and Koʻolau sides of Oʻahu. This knife-edged ridge, which ascends to the summit of Kōnāhuanui (the highest peak of the Koʻolau Range), has two deep notches dug into it, and is visible from the spur road leading to the Pali lookout.

Exactly when the notches were excavated is not known, but they are probably of prehistoric age. Similar cuts exist on the Pauoa and Waʻahila ridges above Mānoa Valley, which also lead to Kōnāhuanui. The English missionary William Ellis, who visited the Pali in 1823, wrote: "The Pari of Anuanu [sic] was an important position in times of war, and the parties in possession of it were usually masters of the island" (1963:11). According to an account published in the Hawaiian newspaper *Ka Naʻi ʻAupuni* in 1906, the notched ridge was used by the army of Oʻahu chief Kalanikupule in 1795, during his unsuccessful attempt to thwart the invading forces of Kamehameha I. Two European cannon were positioned in the notches: "The two cannons of Kalanikupule on the top of the *pali* fired, and the shots fell below on the soldiers of Kamehameha" (Sterling and Summers 1978:314). Kamehameha, however, sent a party up Pauoa Ridge and down over Kōnāhuanui to descend upon the cannoneers from above, thereby capturing the guns. With the defeat of Kalanikupule, Kamehameha gained mastery over all of the islands except Kauaʻi.

References: Ellis (1842:16); Kirch (1985:116); McAllister (1933:88); Sterling and Summers (1978:314–315).

Artificial notches cut into the precipitous ridgeline descending from Puʻu Kōnāhuanui and overlooking the Nuʻuanu Pali offered defensive positions for the Oʻahu army against the invading forces of Kamehameha I in 1795.

He'eia Fishpond—its stone wall partly covered by exotic mangroves—is one of the few archaeological features remaining along the shores of heavily urbanized Kāne'ohe Bay.

8. HE'EIA FISHPOND

O'ahu originally boasted at least 184 fishponds, more than any other island. No fewer than 23 of these were situated around the shores of Kāne'ohe Bay, and together with the extensive irrigated taro fields of Waikāne, Waiā-hole, He'eia, and Ha'ikū Valleys, they made the Ko'olau-poko District (extending from Kualoa to Makapu'u) one of the richest lands on O'ahu. Today, most of these ponds have been filled in or destroyed, and only four remain along the Kāne'ohe shoreline. The best preserved is He'eia Fishpond, which can be viewed from the grounds of He'eia State Park.

He'eia pond is of classic *loko kuapā* type, with a massive arc-shaped seawall more than 5,000 feet long, enclosing about 88 acres. Archaeologist J. Gilbert McAllister reported in 1933 that there were four watch-houses on the walls, and several outlets or sluice gates (*mākāhā*). Regrettably, the pond has fallen into disuse in recent years, and mangrove trees have invaded the pond's interior.

Fishponds were typically the special property of ranking chiefs, who reserved for their own use the sweet mullet (*'ama'ama, Mugil cephalis*) and milkfish (*awa, Chanos chanos*) raised in the brackish waters. He'eia Fishpond was no exception; Kamehameha I took the lands of He'eia for himself after his conquest of O'ahu. The lands and fishpond later were under the control of Chief Abner Pākī, and subsequently passed to his daughter, the Princess Bernice Pauahi Bishop. According to a turn-of-the-century account, the Princess herself often frequented He'eia, where she would entertain parties of her friends, who doubtless partook of the sweet-fleshed mullet, giving the pond its fame.

References: Kelly (1975); Kikuchi (1976); McAllister (1933:173; pl. 4A); Sterling and Summers (1978:198); Summers (1964).

9. ULUPŌ HEIAU

Ulupō Heiau lies in the heart of Kailua *ahupua'a*, on the slopes of Kawainui Marsh (formerly a great fishpond), with a commanding view of the entire region. Although not the largest temple site on O'ahu in terms of area (see Pu'uomahuka, Site 11), Ulupō ("night inspiration") may be the greatest in terms of the sheer mass and volume of stones used in its construction. The temple foundation consists of a nearly square terraced platform, about 140 feet across, with a facing height of more than 30 feet. Standing at the base of this great stone mound, one can vividly appreciate the command that Hawaiian chiefs exercised over their people. Little is known of the history of Ulupō, and there have not been any modern archaeological excavations or dating carried out on it. Thrum, an early student of *heiau*, reported that "Ulupō is one of the famed temples of structure so ancient as to be credited to the Menehunes, and, as usual, with stones brought from long distance passed from hand to hand" (in Sterling and Summers 1978:233). Indeed, the stone-paved pathway leading across the platform is known as the "Menehune pathway."

A feature of special note at Ulupō Heiau is a small spring situated just beyond the base of the massive northwest facing. This spring was enclosed by a stone retaining wall, creating a small pool of clear water about three feet in diameter. According to an old resident of the area, pigs destined for sacrifice on the altar of Ulupō were first brought to this pool to be washed (Sterling and Summers 1978:233).

The *heiau* platform commands a superb view of the adjacent Kawainui Marsh, which some two thousand years ago was an open saltwater embayment. After the sand bar formed along what is today Kailua, the bay become cut off from the sea, and was used by the Hawaiians as a fishpond. The inner shores of the marsh were also used for irrigated taro cultivation.

References: McAllister (1933:186–188); Sterling and Summers (1978:232–234).

The stone-lined spring at the base of the Ulupō Heiau platform was reputedly used to wash the bodies of pigs destined for sacrifice.

The massive stone terrace facing of Ulupō Heiau rises more than thirty feet above the surrounding ground.

10. KŪKANILOKO

In the heart of Oʻahu, on the broad, central plateau between the Koʻolau and Waiʻanae Ranges, lies one of the most famous places for giving birth to chiefs of the highest rank in the entire island chain. Kūkaniloko lies within the district of Waialua, near Kaukonahua Gulch (the site can be approached off Highway 80 at the junction with Whitmore Road). Kūkaniloko has no artificial stone constructions, consisting rather of a group of natural stones partly buried in the red Wahiawā clay. Deeply weathered through the millennia by wind and rain, the stones exhibit smoothed and sculptured surfaces that in some instances resemble miniaturized representations of the Koʻolau *pali*. This unique cluster of boulders, standing eerily alone on the earthen plain, must have caught the attention of ancient Hawaiian sojourners crossing the plateau from ʻEwa to Waialua.

The nineteenth-century Hawaiian sage Samuel Kamakau recorded the ancient tradition of the origins of Kūkaniloko:

> A line of stones was set up on the right hand and another on the left hand, facing north. There sat thirty-six chiefs. There was a backrest, a *kuapuʻu*, on the upper side, this was the rock Kūkaniloko, which was the rock to lean against. If a chiefess entered and leaned against Kūkaniloko and rested on the supports to hold up the thighs in observance of the Līloe *kapu* [the prescribed regulations for birthing], the child born in the presence of the chiefs was called an *aliʻi*, an *akua*, a *wela*—a chief, a god, a blaze of heat (1991:38).

Closely associated with Kūkaniloko was the nearby *heiau* of Hoʻolono-pahu (now destroyed), where the child was taken after birth to have its navel cord cut. Kamakau reports that while the sacred drum Hāwea was beaten, great throngs of commoners (*makaʻāinana*) would gather at a distance, on the eastern side of the valley.

Kūkaniloko was the main birthing place for the Nanaʻulu line of chiefs, and many famous chiefs were born there, including Māʻili-kūkahi, Kākuhihewa, Laʻa (who sailed with the great voyager chief Moʻikeha to Kahiki), and Kapawa. Kapawa is famous in Hawaiian legend for having been deposed by the foreign priest Pāʻao, who introduced human sacrifice to the islands (see Site 50, Wahaʻula Heiau). In a symbolic attempt to

The ancient stones of Kūkaniloko—some of which display petroglyphs—continue to receive offerings, such as this modern fishhook, pineapple, fruit, and lei.

reenact the imposition of Hawaiʻi Island hegemony over the ancient Nanaʻulu line of Oʻahu chiefs, Kamehameha I greatly desired to have his wife—the *kapu* Maui chiefess Keōpūolani—give birth to his heir Liholiho at Kūkaniloko. An illness that befell Keōpūolani, however, prevented the desired event from occurring.

Today, Kūkaniloko and the other stones stand amidst a grove of trees surrounded by acres of pineapple plantation. The site's sacred status remains, however, and it is regularly visited by persons who leave sweet potato, taro, *kī*-leaf lei, and other offerings, perhaps entreating the ancient gods to bestow blessings on their own offspring.

References: Kamakau (1991:38, 53, 68, 105, 136); McAllister (1933:134–137); Kirch and Sahlins (1992, Vol. II:22–24); Sterling and Summers (1978:138–140).

Naturally weathered stones at Kūkaniloko on the central plateau of Oʻahu were the focus of a sacred place for giving birth to high chiefs.

The upper court of Puʻuoma-huka Heiau is enclosed by a low wall and terrace. The equally expansive lower court lies out of view and downslope.

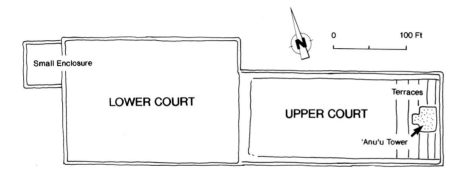

Plan of Puʻuomahuka Heiau (Site 11), based on the survey by McAllister (1933).

11. PU'UOMAHUKA HEIAU, PŪPŪKEA

Commanding a ridge crest north of Waimea Bay, Pu'uomahuka ("hill-of-escape") Heiau boasts one of the most spectacular settings of any *heiau* in the islands, illustrating the principle of situating major temples in prominent positions on the landscape. From the Pu'uomahuka altar, not only could the priests and high chiefs keep watch on Waimea Bay and the river mouth (landing place of Captain Vancouver's supply ship *Daedalus* in 1794), but their gaze encompassed the whole of Waialua District as far as Ka'ena Point. Today the *heiau* is approached from Pūpūkea Road, and is protected as a national landmark within a State historic park.

According to Thrum (1923:30), who gleaned much important traditional information on O'ahu *heiau*, the construction of Pu'uomahuka was credited to the "mythical Menehunes, and the fierceness of its dedicatory fires warmed the hills of Kauai." The architectural design and geographical prominence of the temple, as well as its massive size (in area, it is the largest *heiau* on O'ahu Island), leave no doubt that it functioned as a *luakini* or *heiau po'okanaka*, a war temple at which the ruling chief and his *kahuna nui* would offer human sacrifices to Kū. Thrum identifies the temple with Kaopulupulu, the famous *kahuna* to Kahahana, sacred high chief of O'ahu who was ultimately overthrown by the Maui chief Kahekili in about 1783. Important temples were frequently added to, refurbished, and rededicated and thus accumulated long histories of use; Kaopulupulu was probably only the last of many high priests to officiate at Pu'uomahuka.

Pu'uomahuka is linked with a tragic episode in the history of relations between Hawaiians and foreigners: the killing on May 12, 1792, of three crew members of the *Daedalus*, a supply ship attached to Captain George Vancouver's expedition. Ship's Commander Lieutenant Richard Hergest, William Gooch the astronomer, and a Portuguese sailor known only as Manuel were set upon by a party of *pahupū* warriors while watering the ship at Waimea. The *pahupū*, famous for being tattooed completely over half of their bodies (including the insides of their eyelids), were fiercely loyal to the conquering Maui chief Kahekili. According to Hawaiian traditions of the event, the bodies of Hergest and Gooch were offered up as sacrifices at Pu'uomahuka Heiau. Historian Greg Dening (1988) provides a fascinating account of the *Daedalus* incident and its aftermath.

Measuring roughly 575 feet long and 170 feet wide, Pu'uomahuka manifests the monumental scale of the most important *luakini heiau* in the islands. Architecturally, the temple consists of two main courts, each surrounded by stone walls, with a third, smaller enclosure added on the downslope end. The higher, narrower court was originally well paved with fine, water-rolled gravel carried in basket loads from Waimea Stream, three hundred feet below the temple. Numerous slabs of sandstone are also incorporated in the walls, and these were doubtless obtained along the seashore at Pūpūkea. The altar was situated at the eastern end of the upper court, while a series of stepped terraces flank a rectangular platform that supported the oracle tower. The wider, lower court contains a maze of small, crudely built walls and irregular enclosures; the function of these interior structures is enigmatic.

Pu'uomahuka continues to be used as a place of offerings, with *kī* leaves and fruit frequently placed on the altar. Unfortunately, the modern practice of wrapping *kī* leaves in stones has resulted in considerable rearrangement of the *heiau* paving and facings.

References: McAllister (1933:147–150, fig. 50); Sterling and Summers (1978:142–144).

12. KĀNEʻĀKĪ HEIAU, MĀKAHA VALLEY

Kāneʻākī Heiau holds considerable significance in Hawaiian archaeology for several reasons. Thanks to careful archaeological excavations directed by Ed Ladd for the Bishop Museum in 1969–70, Kāneʻākī is one of only a few *heiau* for which an actual sequence of construction and architectural history are available. After the excavations were completed, the site was restored more or less to its final construction stage, and the perishable wood-and-thatch superstructures and a wooden image of Kū were accurately reconstructed. At Kāneʻākī one can learn both how *heiau* were built and enlarged over time, and the layout of a functioning *heiau*.

Kāneʻākī is situated about midway up the Mākaha Valley in Waiʻanae District. The Bishop Museum's archaeological surveys in Mākaha demonstrated that the *heiau* is part of an extensive complex of habitation sites and agricultural fields, and that the interior parts of the this valley were densely occupied in the late Expansion and Proto-Historic Periods. At the time of European contact, Kāneʻākī is believed to have functioned as a *luakini* or war temple dedicated to the god Kū. This is suggested by the temple's architectural plan, which incorporates two main courtyards, one elevated higher than the other. At the northern or inland end of the higher court are a series of faced terraces defining the altar. Based on evidence obtained during archaeological excavation, Ladd and his team reconstructed two oracle towers (*ʻanuʻu*) on these terraces, flanking a replicated image (*kiʻi*) of the god Kū. In front of the Kū image is an offering stand (*lele*) supported on four posts. Here would be placed offerings such as roasted pigs, bananas, coconuts, and—in times of certain ceremonies performed on behalf of sacred chiefs —a human sacrifice. Hawaiian scholar S. M. Kamakau described such an offering scene: "The burnt offerings were then placed on the *lele* altar. The human sacrifice and the pigs were laid face downward, the man's arm

This accurate replica of a Kū temple image, based on a surviving original in the Bishop Museum, has recently had offerings of *kī*-leaf-wrapped stones placed before it.

Kāneʻākī Heiau in the Mākaha Valley, originally built as a small agricultural temple, was rededicated as a *luakini*-class temple in late prehistory.

embracing a pig on each side, and bunches of coconuts and bananas were laid on the right and left" (1976:144). Two thatched houses are also reconstructed on the upper courtyard: the open-sided structure is a *hale pahu*, or drum house, while the fully enclosed house is the *hale mana*.

The physical appearance of Kāneʻākī in about the 1790s—as reconstructed at the site today—was only the last in six stages of construction that took place over a period of about 275 years. The practice of enlarging and rededicating an existing *heiau* was common; careful archaeological excavation of a temple foundation can reveal the architectural history of such sites. However, such excavations have only been undertaken on a few *heiau* (see Sites 21, 25, and 46), including Kāneʻākī. The first construction phase at Kāneʻākī began about A.D. 1545, as determined by radiocarbon dating of charcoal associated with the oldest structural component. This was a simple stone-faced terrace or platform, now the base for the lower courtyard. At this early time the *heiau* probably functioned as an agricultural temple, or *heiau hoʻoūluʻai;*

similar terraced sites have been found in other parts of the valley dating to the Expansion Period. In the second through fifth construction stages, the original *heiau* platform was gradually enlarged and elaborated. The upper walled court and altar area were finally added in the sixth stage, at which time archaeologist Ed Ladd believes that the temple was rededicated as a *luakini* or war *heiau*. Visitors to the site should note that the modern entrance steps into the temple are not part of the original design, but were opened up by the archaeologist in order to exhibit some of the older, internal architectural features revealed by the excavations.

Note: At the time this book was in preparation, Kāneʻākī Heiau was accessible to the public, but visiting hours were restricted, and prior arrangements must be made. Information on visiting hours and conditions can be obtained by calling the Sheraton Makaha Resort (808-695-9511).

References: Green (1980); Kirch (1985:118, 264–265, fig. 227); Ladd (1973); McAllister (1933:119, fig. 39); Sterling and Summers (1978:77-78).

The *hale manu* and *hale pahu* houses, *lele* offering stand, *ʻanuʻu* towers, and a wooden image of Kū were reconstructed by the Bishop Museum on the upper court of Kāneʻākī Heiau.

Upright stone columns, such as this one at Ke-aīwa Heiau, generally represented particular deities.

13. KE-AĪWA HEIAU, ʻAIEA

Situated in the cool uplands of ʻAiea at a thousand feet above sea level, Ke-aīwa ("the mysterious") Heiau functioned as a *heiau hoʻōla*, where priests (*kahuna lapaʻau*) skilled in the arts of healing and medicinal plants officiated. Unfortunately, little traditional information regarding the site is known, although it is reputed to have been built in the time of the high chief Kākuhihewa. *Kahuna lapaʻau* were highly regarded members of Hawaiian society, whose extensive knowledge of the plant kingdom included the medicinal and healing properties of hundreds of species. According to several scholars who have studied the *lapaʻau* practices, "Under the old cultural order, the art of compounding remedies was practiced by medicine experts as a distinct profession or as a phase of general priesthood" (Handy, Pukui, and Livermore 1934:16). The name Ke-aīwa derives from such a *kahuna lapaʻau* who practiced at this *heiau*, and alludes to his "mysterious" healing powers.

The *heiau* structure comprises a rectangle measuring 100 by 160 feet, with well-built stone walls averaging 4 feet high and 5 feet across. Unfortunately, the site was heavily damaged during the sugar plantation era, prior to being rededicated as a part of the Ke-aīwa Heiau State Recreation Area in 1951. During the reconstruction process, a number of internal structural features were added that were not a part of the original plan (as recorded by archaeologist J. Gilbert McAllister in 1930). These added features include the low circular platforms in the courtyard; only the low dividing wall near the eastern end of the temple is of original design.

References: McAllister (1933:103, fig. 32); Sterling and Summers (1978:11–12).

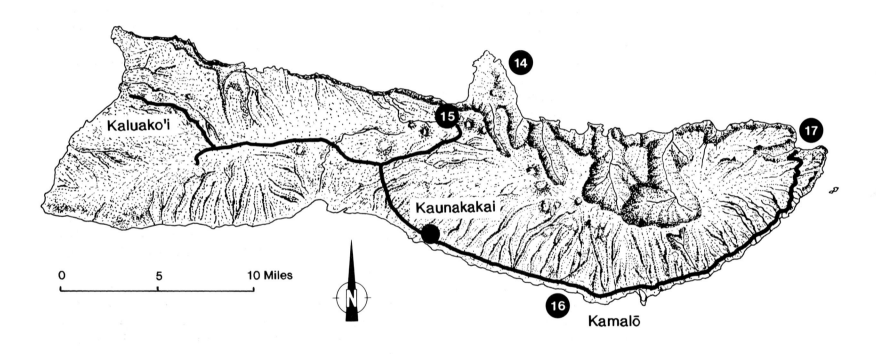

Kaluako'i

14

15

17

Kaunakakai

16

Kamalō

0   5   10 Miles

N

MOLOKAʻI ISLAND

Less than half the area of Kauaʻi, the long but narrow island of Molokaʻi ranks fifth in size. Lava flows from two volcanic shields formed the island some one and a half to two million years ago, the larger and higher eastern volcano rising to an elevation of 4,961 feet at Kamakou. These high mountains cause a rain shadow that creates much drier conditions on the lower western end, with its 1,381-foot summit of Puʻu Nānā. Long after the main mountains were formed and their volcanoes had become extinct, a later eruption along the windward coastline built the peninsula of Kalaupapa, location of the famous leper colony and home of Father Damien for many years (see Site 14).

Adapting to the strong ecological contrasts between the well-watered eastern and the arid western parts of the island, the majority of the Hawaiian population in pre-contact times lived in the east. The windward district of Koʻolau comprised the four great valleys of Waikolu, Pelekunu, Wailau, and Hālawa. With their fast-flowing streams and alluvial soils, these valleys boasted extensive wet taro cultivation. Of these windward valleys, only Hālawa is accessible by car. Hālawa Valley is also the location of the earliest known settlement on the island, dating to the Developmental Period (ca. A.D. 600). The Kona District was well populated, especially around Pūkoʻo and Wailua, and several massive *heiau* platforms still exist in this region. The western half of Molokaʻi was traditionally known as Kaluakoʻi (literally, "the adz pit"), renowned for its many sources and quarries of fine-grained basalt rock prized for the manufacture of adzes and other tools. Sweet potatoes were cultivated on the summit regions of Maunaloa, but most people in Kaluakoʻi lived in smaller fishing hamlets dispersed around the coastline.

Molokaʻi, lying between Oʻahu and Maui (although it is much closer to the latter), was under the political domination of both Oʻahu and Maui chiefs at various times in its prehistory. With a small population base, the Molokaʻi chiefs could not outcompete the more powerful Maui and Oʻahu forces. However, the Molokaʻi people developed their own forms of resistance to domination, most notably the arts of sorcery. One of the most famous of all *kahuna*, Lanikaula, made his abode deep within the *kukui* grove at Puʻu-o-Hoku on the island's eastern tip. And, the greatly feared sorcery gods called the Kalaipāhoa were carved from the wood of trees taken from the summit of Maunaloa in Kaluakoʻi District.

In recent times, Molokaʻi has been largely spared the development that has transformed the landscapes of other islands. Ranching, and for a time, pineapple cultivation, have been the island's main economic activities, and population stands at only a little more than six thousand people. Molokaʻi—especially the east end—remains a strong center of traditional Hawaiian culture and values. The relative lack of land development has preserved much of the island's rich archaeological landscape. However, most sites lie on private land and are not accessible to the public. The few sites that are open, however, are well worth visiting and include one of the most extensive fishpond complexes in the islands (Site 16), and the vast stone-faced irrigation fields and habitation sites of the Hālawa Valley (Site 17). In a dramatic setting high above the cliffs overlooking Kalaupapa Peninsula is also Kauleo-nānāhoa, the "phallic rock" (Site 15).

Map of Molokaʻi Island.

14. KALAUPAPA PENINSULA

Kalaupapa: the very name could strike fear into the heart of a nineteenth-century Hawaiian. For it was to this remote, windswept peninsula on the northern Moloka'i coast, lying under the shadow of forbidding 4,000-foot high cliffs, that those who had contracted the dread *ma'i pākē*, leprosy, were banished for life. The Hawaiian government established Kalaupapa as a leper colony in 1865, and some sufferers of Hansen's disease remain there today (at their own will), although no new patients have been admitted since 1969. The story of Kalaupapa, and of Father Damien—the Catholic priest who arrived in 1873 and spent sixteen years of his life improving the lot of the colony's occupants—has become world renowned through books and film. Kalaupapa is administered by the State of Hawaii Health Department, while the peninsula and its unique historic and prehistoric sites are being transferred to the National Park Service (Kalaupapa National Historical Park was established by an act of Congress in 1980). At the present time, Kalaupapa can only be visited by making arrangements with one of the local tour operators authorized to escort visitors.

Whereas the modern Hansen's disease settlement and clinic is situated on the western side of the peninsula (in the *ahupua'a* of Kalaupapa), the original settlement in Father Damien's time was on the eastern side, at Kalawao. (A third *ahupua'a*, Makanalua, occupies the middle section of the peninsula, and includes the volcanic crater of Kauhakō, from which the lavas creating the peninsula were erupted.) No one lives at Kalawao today, but Damien's exquisite little church—Siloama—stands amidst a cluster of Hawaiian graves. Nearby are the ruins of the old settlement: stone enclosure walls, house foundations, and on the former grounds of the Baldwin Home for Boys, the stone and lime-plaster foundations of the kitchen.

Although known to most people primarily through its historical connections with Father Damien and the leper colony, Kalaupapa also boasts a rich prehistory and numerous archaeological sites. The area has yet to be thoroughly surveyed archaeologically, but more than sixteen *heiau* and shrines, a *hōlua* slide, habitation caves, numerous house sites, and extensive dryland agricultural fields are recorded. The gently sloping lands surrounding Kauhakō Crater were ideally suited to sweet-potato culti-

vation, and parallel stone rows resulting from intensive gardening can be seen over much of this land. Some of these fields date from the mid-nineteenth century, when Kalaupapa witnessed a "boom" in the export of sweet potatoes, in response to the demand for food from the San Francisco Gold Rush of 1849.

A detailed understanding of the prehistory of Kalaupapa Peninsula must await more archaeological research. However, test excavations in one lava tube habitation cave by a University of Hawai'i team in 1966–67 revealed that the peninsula has been occupied for as long as a thousand years. The many *heiau*, some quite large, also offer mute testimony to Kalaupapa's former wealth and the extent of its population.

References: Daws (1973); Summers (1971:188–196).

A weathered gravestone in the cemetery behind Father Damien's Siloama Church at Kalaupapa.

Four-thousand-foot cliffs provide a spectacular backdrop for the facing stones of an ancient *heiau* at Kalaupapa. Only the large foundation stones remain, the bulk of the temple foundation having been robbed to construct pasture enclosures during the nineteenth century.

One of several *heiau* platforms to be found on the
inland slopes of Kalaupapa
Peninsula.

The isolated peninsula
of Kalaupapa affords
spectacular views of
the windward coast of
Moloka'i, indented by
Waikolu, Pelekunu, and
Wailau valleys.

15. KAULEONĀNĀHOA, THE PHALLIC STONE

Perched just below the summit of Nānāhoa Hill, and formerly visible prominently on the skyline for many miles distant, is the large stone Kauleonānāhoa ("the penis of Nānāhoa"). Today a dense grove of ironwood trees planted during a reforestation project shades the stone, which is approached from a trail leading west from the Kalaupapa lookout parking area. This rock is probably the finest example in the archipelago of a class of "phallic stones," usually natural rock formations with occasional artificial modifications. Kauleonānāhoa appears to be a natural geological formation, although pioneer archaeologist John F. G. Stokes detected traces of artificial working "on the blunt ridge underneath the head." There is also a female stone farther down the slope of Nānāhoa Hill, for which at least three names have been recorded: Kawahuna, Nawaʻakaluli, and Waihuʻehuʻe.

Stones such as Kauleonānāhoa were thought to embody the male creative principle, and were often associated with the creator god Kāne (in which case they were called *pōhaku o Kāne*). Naturally elongated stones, especially those of angular dykestone or of beach stone that had been thoroughly rounded and polished by the sea, were often set upright within shrines and *heiau*.

Archaeologist Stokes and other explorers in the early 1900s found several small engraved stones near Kauleonānāhoa that were carved to resemble female genitals. The great Hawaiian scholar Mary Kawena Pukui related to Catherine Summers that these stones were taken to Nānāhoa to receive the *mana* or creative power of the place; they would then be taken home to make the land fertile and crops productive (Summers 1971:30).

Boulders clustered to the north and northeast of Kauleonānāhoa are carved with more than twenty-four petroglyphs. The figures depicted are primarily human, and are quite shallowly engraved into the stone.

References: Summers (1971:28–31).

Petroglyphs pecked into a boulder near Kauleonānāhoa (Site 15), after Summers (1971).

Kauleonānāhoa thrusts skyward from the ridgeline overlooking Kalaupapa.

16. SOUTH COAST FISHPONDS

The wall of a small fishpond near Pūkoʻo. On the horizon the islet of Moku Hoʻoniki is silhouetted by the early morning sun.

The gently curving stone-walled arc of a prehistoric fishpond along the southern shore of Molokaʻi Island, constructed from thousands of basalt and coral boulders.

"Fishponds were things that beautified the land, and a land with many fishponds was called 'fat.'" In these words the nineteenth-century scholar Samuel Kamakau (1976:47) captured the essence of aquaculture in Hawaiian civilization. No land has more fishponds, nor as many romantic coastline views of ponds, as the southern shore of Molokaʻi. (Oʻahu originally had more ponds in number than any other island, but a great many of these have been filled in or destroyed.) At least seventy-three ponds were constructed along this protected leeward shore between Kolo in the west and Kanahā in the east. Many of these fishponds are readily viewed from Kamehameha V Highway, running eastward from Kaunakakai town.

Among the indigenous people of the Pacific Islands, only the Hawaiians developed true aquaculture by using ponds to husband fish, as opposed to merely trapping

fish with weirs. Hawaiian fishponds, *loko iʻa*, were primarily used to raise mullet or *ʻamaʻama (Mugil cephalis)* and milkfish or *awa (Chanos chanos)*, both of which thrive in brackish water. A species of small shrimp, *ʻōpae*, was also regularly harvested. The construction of ponds varied depending upon local topography and available materials, but most commonly a semicircular wall of stones would be constructed from one point on the shoreline to another. Such *loko kuapā* ponds enclosed areas ranging from one up to five hundred acres or more. Both volcanic stones from the land and large coral heads from the reef were used to construct the walls, which had to stand two or three feet above the high-tide level. In one or more places these walls were breached with sluice gates (*mākāhā*), permitting seawater to flow back and forth with the tides. Wooden slats allowed the young fry to enter the pond from the sea, but prevented the mature fish from escaping. Fish were periodically harvested, usually by hauling large seine nets.

Construction of a *loko kuapā* required substantial labor, and thus ponds were built under the aegis of chiefs who could command the people to haul the thousands of stones necessary to form the long walls. Once constructed, however, ponds were efficiently operated by a small group of specialists, often an extended family who worked the pond for the chief. The bulk of the harvest was reserved for use by the chief and his retainers, with a lesser portion going to the common people.

Most of the Molokaʻi fishponds are of the *loko kuapā* type. A few are still operational, although most have fallen into disuse. At periods of low tide, one can make out the ruins of old ponds whose walls have been broken down by storm waves. The antiquity of fishpond construction in the Hawaiian Islands is not well understood by archaeologists, although it is believed that the majority of ponds were constructed during the Expansion and Proto-Historic Periods (from about A.D. 1100 to European contact).

References: Kikuchi (1976); Kirch (1985: 211–214); Summers (1964; 1971).

17. HĀLAWA VALLEY

Descending the narrow, winding road from Puʻu-o-Hoku Ranch on the eastern end of Molokaʻi, the landscape of lush Hālawa Valley with its spectacular twin waterfalls (Moaʻula and Hīpuapua) is not soon forgotten. An early *haole* explorer to the Islands penned his thoughts of this panorama in 1853:

> The Valley of Halawa . . . is the finest scene on Molokai. The traveler stumbles on its brink un-awares. At a depth of nearly twenty-five hundred feet below him, the whole scene is spread out before him like an exquisite panorama. Several large cascades were leaping from a height of several hundred feet at the head of the valley. Scores of taro beds, and a number of dwellings, and the romantic river, are all seen at a glance (Bates 1854:274–275).

Hālawa Valley was archaeologically investigated in 1969–70 by a team that I co-directed (see Kirch and Kelly 1975). Excavations in the coastal sand dunes near the stream mouth revealed an extensive settlement, radiocarbon-dated to the Developmental Period (A.D. 600–1100), the oldest archaeological site yet discovered on Molokaʻi. The house foundations in this early village site were oval or round ended, and lined with low walls of water-rounded cobbles; inside these low huts were rectangular stone-lined hearths. The early Hawaiians who settled next to the Hālawa stream mouth used highly polished stone adzes with shapes more like the adzes made by their Polynesian relatives in the Marquesas Islands, quite different from the adz types typical in later Hawaiian prehistory. They fished the offshore waters with nets and small bone fishhooks, gathered ʻopihi and hīhīwai shellfish, and raised pigs, dogs, and chickens for food. They also cultivated the nearby hillsides, for charcoal found in erosional layers near the early village site reveals the effects of clearing the valley's native forest in order to plant crops.

Over the centuries, the population of Hālawa grew to perhaps as many as one thousand people, nurtured by the rich agricultural lands. Gradually, the entire valley floor and slopes became densely covered in irrigation canals and taro pondfields, dryland agricultural terraces, house sites, pig pens, and temples of various sorts. Several house sites and agricultural terraces were excavated and radiocarbon-dated by our project in 1969–70, and proved to have been built during the Expansion and Proto-Historic Periods. By the end of the Proto-Historic Period, Hālawa Valley boasted one of the most intensive agricultural landscapes in the islands, with nearly seven hundred irrigated taro fields.

Such great agricultural wealth (for food was truly wealth in ancient Hawaiʻi) also fostered political power, and attracted the attention of mighty chiefs. In the Proto-Historic Period, Molokaʻi became the political spoil of rival war chiefs from Oʻahu and Maui, who fought each other for control of the island. The local Molokaʻi chiefs frequently turned to sorcery to defend themselves, giving the island a reputation (remaining to this day) for the practice of *kahuna ʻanāʻanā*. In Hālawa Valley, two large *luakini heiau* were constructed by conquering chiefs. Mana Heiau, high on the northern slopes, consists of a massive stone platform with a terraced facade rising thirteen feet high in places. Alapaʻinui, a great war chief from Hawaiʻi Island, dedicated Mana Heiau following a war between the Kona and Koʻolau Districts, in which Alapaʻinui came to the aid of the Kona chiefs. Pāpā Heiau, nestled in the side valley of Hālawa Iki, is a complex arrangement of enclosures, platforms, and terraces; the Hālawa people told archaeologist John F. G. Stokes in 1909 that Pāpā Heiau was a sort of "college" for the training of priests or *kahuna*.

Note: Most of the land in Hālawa is privately owned, but two old Hawaiian Government trails (*ala nui*) run up the south and north sides of the valley as far as Moaʻula Falls. (At the time of publication, there was some dispute between landowners and various State and County agencies as to public access to these old *ala nui* trails.) The three-mile round-trip hike, crossing over and past endless walls and terraces, takes one through some of the most intriguing and spectacular archaeological ruins in the islands.

References: Kirch (1985:127–130); Kirch and Kelly (1975); Summers (1971:159–171).

The sheltered bay at Hālawa Valley offered a convenient canoe landing even in stormy weather. Sand dunes at the valley mouth conceal the oldest known occupation deposits on Molokaʻi Island.

A massive boulder near one of the main irrigation canals in Hālawa Valley displays numerous smooth basin-shaped depressions, produced by grinding and sharpening the cutting edges of stone adzes.

A pavement of moss-covered stone slabs once welcomed visitors at the threshold of a house site in the interior of Hālawa Valley.

Carefully constructed stone
facing walls of ancient
irrigated pondfields
crisscross the floor of
Hālawa Valley.

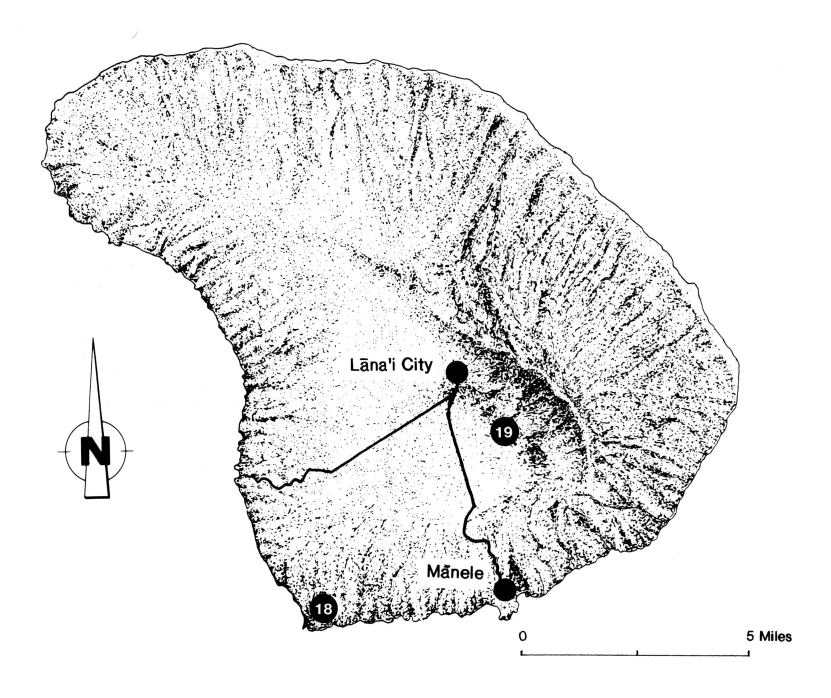

Lāna'i City

19

Mānele

18

N

0   5 Miles

LĀNAʻI ISLAND

With a land area of only 139 square miles, Lānaʻi is the smallest of the accessible main islands (Kahoʻolawe and Niʻihau are smaller yet, but are not generally open to visitors). Formed of a single shield volcano, Lānaʻi rises to a height of just 3,370 feet at the summit of Lānaʻihale. Because of its low elevation, and the fact that it lies in the rain shadow of Maui, Lānaʻi is a rather dry island. Its windward slopes are sliced by a few deep gorges, but the streams in these run only intermittently after heavy rains in the uplands. Only on the mountain crest of Lānaʻihale can some remnant wet forest be found over a limited area.

Because of this overall arid climate, the prehistoric population of Lānaʻi relied primarily on the cultivation of dryland crops, especially sweet potatoes. These were grown mostly in the higher elevation areas, such as the broad expanse of the Pālāwai Basin with its fertile soils and greater rainfall and dew precipitation. Any archaeological sites on the floor of the Pālāwai Basin have been thoroughly destroyed through years of intensive pineapple cultivation in this century, but *heiau*, petroglyphs, an adz quarry, and habitation sites situated around the rim of the Basin indicate that it was formerly a main locus of prehistoric Hawaiian activity.

Throughout most of the twentieth century, Lānaʻi was operated by the Dole Corporation as the largest pineapple plantation in the world. Pineapples are no longer grown there, however, and the island is now being developed as a major resort destination. The owners are working to preserve the island's rich archaeological legacy, which includes the major coastal village complex at Kaunolū (Site 18). This site is one of the finest examples of a well-preserved, integrated settlement to be seen in the Hawaiian Islands, and includes numerous house platforms (including one platform occupied briefly by King Kamehameha I), a massive *heiau*, petroglyphs, and other features. Also accessible on Lānaʻi are the Luahiwa petroglyphs on the lower slopes of Lānaʻihale, a cluster of large boulders with motifs dating to both prehistoric and early historic times.

Because the island of Lānaʻi is privately held, visitors to the island who wish to visit these sites should confirm accessibility and arrangements with local authorities prior to planning a trip.

Map of Lānaʻi Island.

18. KAUNOLŪ VILLAGE

One of the best preserved Proto-Historic Period village sites in the entire Hawaiian Islands lies at the southeastern tip of Lānaʻi, where Kaunolū Bay provided a sheltered landing for fishing canoes. The archaeological ruins occupy the stony ridges on both sides of Kaunolū Gulch, a normally dry streambed subject to flash floods during occasional rainstorms in the uplands. What attracted people to establish a village in these parched surroundings were the rich fishing grounds in the deep waters offshore, under the lee of the thousand-foot high cliffs of the southern Lānaʻi coastline. Fresh water was scarce, however, and had to be obtained from a well sunk into the alluvial sediments of the gulch bottom, tapping the fragile brackish water aquifer.

Kaunolū Village was first studied archaeologically in 1921–22 by pioneering ethnologist Kenneth P. Emory, who made a detailed survey of the *heiau* site, eighty-six house platforms, petroglyphs, and other features. Recently, the site complex has been restudied by the Bishop Museum, and with their assistance the Lānaʻi Company has established an interpretive trail to guide visitors through the ruins.

On the western side of Kaunolū Gulch, Halulu Heiau stands prominently on the cliff edge, its massive stone walls built up high on the northern and western sides. This temple probably functioned as a *luakini*, and Kamehameha I is reputed to have held ceremonies here between 1778 and 1810. Kamehameha evidently enjoyed residing and fishing at Kaunolū, and the king's own house platform lies directly across the gulch from Halulu Heiau on the eastern bank. A stone *kūʻula* or fish god, with the proper name of Kunihi, formerly stood on a stone altar in the gulch, directly below the *heiau*. This image was removed and hidden away by Ohua, the last

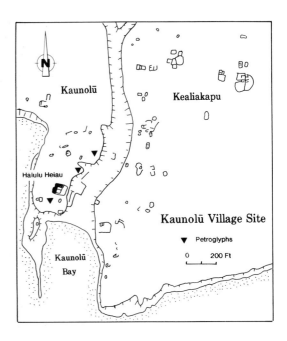

Plan of archaeological features at the Kaunolū village site (Site 18), based on the map by Emory (1924).

Halulu Heiau, perched on the western edge of Kaunolū Gulch, was the setting for rituals performed by Kamehameha I and other ruling chiefs.

man to live in Kaunolū Village, on the order of King Kamehameha V in 1868.

Numerous petroglyphs pecked into boulder surfaces can be seen in several areas on the western ridge, both seaward and inland of Halulu Heiau. Many of these petroglyphs are finely executed, the anthropomorphic figures having "muscular" limbs filled in by pecking. A number of "bird-man" motifs, human bodies with avian heads or beaks, are also present at Kaunolū.

West of Halulu Heiau, at the very edge of the precipice, is a notch in the lava ridge known as "Kahekili's Leap." Kahekili, the ruling chief of Maui and arch-rival of Kamehameha, controlled Lāna'i in the late 1700s and is said to have made his warriors leap through this notch and plunge into the sea below as a test of their courage.

The main village area lies on the eastern side of Kaunolū Gulch, an area properly known as Keāliakapu.

Dispersed over this terrain are numerous habitation complexes, consisting of dwelling platforms and terraces, walled enclosures, and other structures. A small lava tube shelter, Ulaula Cave, is also located here, and was archaeologically excavated by Emory in the 1950s, yielding a collection of bone trolling lure points of the kind used by the ancient Hawaiians to catch 'ahi, aku, and other pelagic game fish.

Note: Access to Kaunolū Village is controlled by the Lāna'i Company, which owns the site (808-565-3000). Tours may be arranged with either of the two hotels operated by the Lāna'i Company; the very rough road to the site is for four-wheel-drive vehicles only, and is off-limits to any rental vehicles.

References: Emory (1924:51–60, 97–103, pls. IV, IX, X); Kirch (1985:134, figs. 118, 199).

Numerous petroglyphs are shallowly pecked or incised on boulder faces at Kaunolū.

19. PETROGLYPHS AT LUAHIWA

Lāna'i Island resembles somewhat a gigantic stone mortar, with an extensive central depression—the Pālāwai Basin ("putrid water")—which until recently formed the largest pineapple plantation in the world. Sweet potatoes were the crop favored by the ancient Hawaiians, and they evidently flourished in Pālāwai Basin's volcanic soils. On the steep slopes rising up from the Pālāwai flatlands to the ridge crest of Lāna'ihale, a number of archaeological sites attest to Hawaiian occupation and use of the area. These include a quarry for extracting fine-grained basalt for stone adz making, and at Luahiwa, a major petroglyph site.

The Luahiwa petroglyphs were carved on a group of twenty large basalt boulders arranged over the hillside. The use of boulder surfaces for petroglyphs is common on Lāna'i (see Site 18), as it is also on Moloka'i, in contrast with the use of vertical cliff faces on Maui and flat pahoehoe lava surfaces on Hawai'i. Pioneer archaeologist Kenneth P. Emory, who surveyed the site in 1921, wrote that "Nowhere on Lanai is there such a variety of forms or such a crowding of old and new petroglyphs or so many examples of stratification" (1924:95). By "stratification," Emory referred to the complex overlayering and cross-cutting of figures evident on some of the boulders. Cox and Stasack carefully analyzed the pattern of overlapping figures on one large Luahiwa boulder (1970:50–51, fig. 73), unraveling at least four stages of petroglyph carving. The earliest figures are mostly triangular-bodied human forms. Later figures that cut into and over the earlier motifs include themes dating to the postcontact period, such a man mounted on a horse and another figure holding a gun, as well as several dogs with curly tails.

Note: The Luahiwa petroglyphs are somewhat off the beaten track, accessible from a dirt road that is passable by car when dry. The site lies on the property of the Lāna'i Company, and permission to visit the site should first be obtained from the Lāna'i Company management (808-565-3000), or by inquiring at one of the two principal hotels on the island.

Reference: Cox with Stasack (1970:90); Emory (1924:94–97, pl. VII–VIII).

The petroglyphs at Luahiwa are carved into a cluster of large, weathered boulders scattered over the hill slope.

Petroglyphs on a boulder at Luahiwa include human forms and a dog with a curved tail.

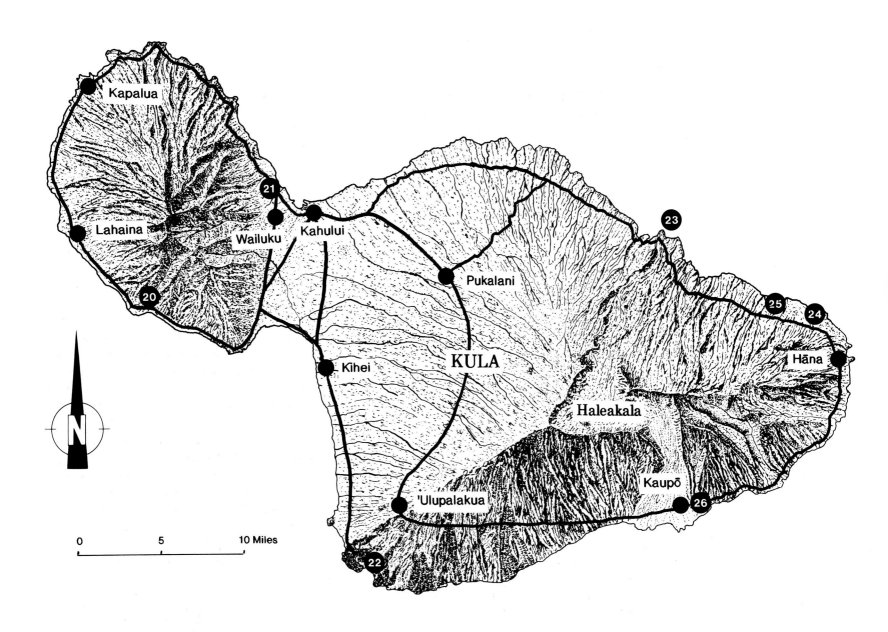

Kapalua

21

Lahaina

Wailuku

Kahului

20

Pukalani

KULA

25

24

Hāna

Kihei

Haleakala

'Ulupalakua

Kaupō

26

22

N

0　　　　5　　　　10 Miles

MAUI ISLAND

Geologically speaking, Maui consists of two islands—each formed by a separate volcanic mountain—joined as one land mass by a broad isthmus of coalescing lava flows. West Maui is older, its volcanic activity having ceased about one million years ago. Consequently, the West Maui mountains (reaching their summit at 5,788 feet on Puʻu Kukui) are heavily weathered, radiating streams having eroded spectacularly deep gorges, such as ʻĪao Valley. In contrast, the younger mass of East Maui with its lofty crater, Haleakalā (elevation 10,023 feet), has undergone only relatively minor weathering, primarily on the windward coast (the Hāna and Kīpahulu areas). In the leeward parts of East Maui, such as Kahikinui and Kula, the volcanic slopes have been only slightly incised by streams. East Maui is technically a dormant rather than an extinct volcano, having last erupted in A.D. 1790.

Traditionally, Maui was divided into twelve districts. On West Maui, Wailuku District (where the present county seat is located) encompassed the windward valleys of ʻĪao, Waiheʻe, and Waiehu with their rich agricultural lands and irrigated fields. The impressive *heiau* complex of Halekiʻi–Pihana (Site 21) is situated here. The leeward districts of Kāʻanapali and Lahaina were dependent more on dry farming. In the early nineteenth century, Lahaina for a time was the capital of the Hawaiian Kingdom and a major port for the North Pacific whaling fleet. The old town contains important historic buildings, as well as the archaeological remnants of a brick palace constructed for Kamehameha I between 1798 and 1802. Outside of Lahaina town can be found the petroglyph complex at Olowalu (Site 20), where the rock art was incised on a vertical cliff facing.

On the vast western slopes of Haleakalā, the Kula District was a major zone of intensive dryland cultivation, primarily of sweet potatoes and taro, and in some places the pattern of the old Hawaiian field system, with its walls and borders, can be discerned in the modern ranch pastureland (as in the area immediately northwest of ʻUlupalakua Ranch). Kula was densely populated in late prehistory, but many of the archaeological features here have been obliterated or destroyed by modern developments. The ancient districts of Honuaʻula and Kahikinui encompass the most arid, leeward parts of East Maui. Within Honuaʻula is the important coastal fishing village site of Keoneʻōʻio (Site 22). The district of Kaupō, with its great gap opening into Haleakalā Crater, is transitional to the windward district of Kīpahulu, noteworthy for its deep valleys and waterfalls, some of which plunge directly into the sea. At the boundary between Kaupō and Kīpahulu is the point of land called Moku-lau, setting for the ruins of an early historic school and settlement (Site 26).

The windward coast and slopes of East Maui were divided into four districts: Hāmākua Poko, Hāmākua Loa, Koʻolau, and Hāna. Within Koʻolau District lies Keʻanae Peninsula (Site 23), famous for its irrigated taro fields, still in cultivation today by the local Hawaiian community. Hāna District contains the great *luakini* war temple of Piʻilanihale (Site 25), the largest stone monument known in Hawaiian archaeology. Also located here is Waiʻānapanapa State Park, which includes a fine example of a smaller *ahupuaʻa* temple (Site 24).

Map of Maui Island.

20. PETROGLYPHS AT OLOWALU

The *ahupua'a* of Olowalu—on the dry, leeward side of West Maui near the famous early capital of Lahaina—is infamous in Hawaiian history as the scene of a gruesome massacre that occurred in A.D. 1790. Captain Simon Metcalfe of the trading ship *Eleanora*, angered at the theft of a small boat, fired cannon and musket shot broadside into scores of canoes, killing more than one hundred Hawaiians. Today, the hot plains of Olowalu are carpeted in fields of sugarcane, grown by the Pioneer Mill Company of Lahaina. Some distance inland, near the mouth of Olowalu Valley, is a small but conspicuous hill called Kīlea, with a vertical cliff face exhibiting a complex of petroglyphs.

The petroglyphs at Olowalu—as with most on the Island of Maui—were pecked into vertical cliff surfaces, quite a different medium from the pahoehoe lava surfaces used, for example, at most Hawai'i Island sites (see Sites 33, 35, and 49). The petroglyphs are only shallowly engraved into the dense basalt forming the Olowalu cliff: "The surfaces have a patina that can be knocked away by bruising, which tends to produce broad, unformalized, rough-edged images" (Cox with Stasack 1970:10).

The functions and meanings of petroglyphs in ancient Hawaiian culture are enigmatic, but have been the subject of considerable speculation and theorizing.

Cox and Stasack, whose exhaustive study of petroglyphs remains the key authoritative work, thought that petroglyphs served as visual images and symbols related to: "(1) Recording of trips and communication concerning other events, on trails and at boundaries; (2) A concern for insuring long life and personal well being; and (3) The commemoration of events and legends" (1970:13).

The Olowalu petroglyphs were finely executed, and include a variety of human representations (many with triangular body forms), dogs, and sails. Sails depict the classic Hawaiian "crab-claw" shape, with individual sewn sections of *lau hala (Pandanus)* matting. Altogether, there are about a hundred individual glyph units on the cliff face at Olowalu. Unfortunately, there has been some damage to the site by unscrupulous visitors who have added their own graffiti to the rock faces.

Note: At one time the Olowalu petroglyph site was well marked, and a viewing platform existed. After some vandalism occurred, however, the roadside sign and platform were removed. Permission to visit the site must now be obtained by calling the Pioneer Mill Company (in Lahaina), whose cane-hauling road must be traversed; visitors who do not obtain prior permission may be subject to trespass charges.

Reference: Cox with Stasack (1970:93).

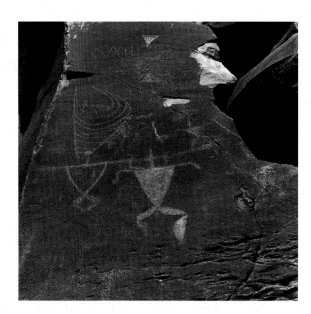

Several human figures and a "crab-claw" sail motif on the sheer cliff face at Olowalu. Modern graffiti have unfortunately marred the site.

Perhaps one of the most dramatic rock-art sites in the islands, the Olowalu petroglyphs were incised into the sheer cliff walls.

The stone terraces of Haleki`i Heiau were constructed to take advantage of the natural high sandstone ridge overlooking `Īao Stream.

The platform and walled enclosures of Haleki`i Heiau were constructed of smooth, rounded cobbles and boulders hauled up to the ridgetop site from nearby `Īao Stream.

21. HALEKI'I–PIHANA HEIAU

Straddling the low ridge immediately west of 'Īao Stream in Wailuku are two imposing *heiau*, Haleki'i ("house of images") and Pihana, preserved together by the State of Hawaii Parks Division. These were both *luakini heiau* with important traditional linkages to famous chiefs. Pihana is reputed to have been built by Ki'ihewa, a chief who lived in the time of Kaka'e; the *heiau* was rededicated by Liholiho, son and heir of Kamehameha I, after his father's unification of the Kingdom in the early historic period. Haleki'i Heiau is said to have been constructed by the chief Kihapi'ilani.

Aside from their traditional associations and importance as well-preserved architectural examples of massive *luakini* class *heiau*, Haleki'i and Pihana are of archaeological note because they are among a very few temples to have been carefully excavated and dated. Archaeologist Michael Kolb carried out stratigraphic excavations in both of these temple sites in 1989–90, yielding an architectural construction sequence dated by eleven radiocarbon dates. From these data, Kolb was able to reconstruct the history of *heiau* construction on this lithified sand-dune ridge overlooking the fertile coastal plains of Wailuku, Waihe'e, and Waichu.

The story begins with the construction of a small temple on the site of Pihana sometime between A.D. 1260 and 1400. Between A.D. 1410 and 1640, Pihana was expanded, and part of the site was used as a chiefly residence; this may coincide with the oral tradition of the dedication of Pihana as a *luakini* temple by the chief Ki'ihewa. This second phase also witnessed the first construction at Haleki'i, a flanking terrace along the crest of the sand hill. Both temples underwent major expansions in the period from A.D. 1662 to 1705, when the sites began to take on their present architectural configurations. Kolb estimates that no less than 39,159 labor-days were invested in these building efforts, hauling the large waterworn basalt cobbles up the steep slope from 'Īao Stream to the ridge top, and setting them in position. Large quantities of fine *'ili'ili* river gravel were also brought up by the basket load to pave the terraces and platforms. These monuments testify to the power of the late prehistoric Hawaiian chiefs to direct and command the people within their dominions. The final building episode took place between A.D. 1684 and 1778, and was confined to Pihana Heiau. Interestingly, this final episode involved the reorientation of the *heiau* to face the island of Hawai'i, probably in response to the interchiefdom wars that the Maui chiefs Kekaulike, Kamehamehanui, and Kahekili were fighting with their Hawai'i rivals.

The excavations at Haleki'i and Pihana Heiau demonstrate that Hawaiian stone temple sites, when studied through stratigraphic excavation and with the use of radiocarbon dating, have the potential to yield valuable information on Hawaiian religious and political history. As more of these sites are preserved and studied in the future, our understanding of the development of Hawaiian society and culture will be enhanced.

References: Kamakau (1961:188); Kolb (1991:141–155, 212–223).

A high facing of stacked lava blocks supports a small *heiau* platform at the Keone'ō'io Archaeological District.

An upright *kū'ula* stone within a small *ko'a* or fishing shrine in the Keone'ō'io Archaeological District.

Keone'ō'io Archaeological District includes this fine example of artificial grinding depressions on a pahoehoe lava surface. The depressions were produced in the process of preparing lava abrading tools used in fishhook manufacture.

22. KEONEʻŌʻIO ARCHAEOLOGICAL DISTRICT (LA PÉROUSE BAY)

On May 29, 1786, the French explorer Admiral Jean-François Galaup, Comte de La Pérouse, was sailing his two ships *La Boussole* and *L'Astrolabe* past Hawaiʻi and along the southeastern coastline of Maui. La Pérouse's expedition—whose subsequent disappearance would become one of the great mysteries of the early nineteenth century (it was later proved that the ships were lost on the reefs of Vanikolo in the Solomon Islands during a hurricane)—had been sent by the French government to emulate the great discoveries of Captain James Cook. Off Maui, La Pérouse ordered the anchors dropped outside a rocky bay named Keoneʻōʻio ("bonefish beach"), in the lee of Haleakalā. The Hawaiians "hastened to come up to the ships in their canoes," bringing taro and bananas, *kapa*, and "other curiosities forming part of their attire" (Dunmore, ed., 1994:82). The following morning, the French ventured ashore in four boats with twenty armed soldiers, on guard for the sort of tragedy that had befallen Captain Cook (see Site 45). Despite the military precautions, the French were greeted warmly, La Pérouse being offered a pig and he in return giving "axes and pieces of iron which were for them gifts of inestimable value" (Dunmore, ed., 1994:86). Later that day after returning to his cabin aboard the *Boussole*, La Pérouse penned a brief description of the small hamlets at Keoneʻōʻio :

> The inhabitants drink only a brackish water obtained in shallow wells that yield no more than half a barrel of water a day. On our walk we came upon four small villages of 10 to 12 houses; they are built and roofed with straw [*pili* grass] and resemble those of our poorest peasants, the roofs are coupled, the door is usually situated at the gable end, it is only 3½ feet in height and one has to bend to enter—it consists of a small screen which anyhow can open. Their furnishings are merely mats which, like our carpets, make a very clean floor on which these natives sleep. Their only kitchen utensils are gourds of a large size to which

they give the desired shape when they are still green; they varnish them and paint various designs on them in black (Dunmore, ed., 1994:89).

Today, the archaeological vestiges of these "four small villages" comprise the Keoneʻōʻio Archaeological District, and provide an excellent example of late prehistoric coastal habitation sites, along with associated religious and special-function features. Precisely when Keoneʻōʻio Bay was first settled by the Hawaiians is not known, since no archaeological excavations have yet been undertaken, and there are no radiocarbon dates for the village sites. However, other settlements along the southeast Maui coast date to as early as A.D. 1100. Keoneʻōʻio is associated in oral traditions with the Hawaiʻi Island chiefs Kauholanuimahu and Koi, who may have ruled in the 1400s or 1500s. The Hawaiian scholar S. M. Kamakau wrote that during the wars between Maui and Hawaiʻi Islands in the eighteenth century, the high chief Kalaniʻōpuʻu beached his fleet of war canoes at Keoneʻōʻio, forcing the people to flee into the interior (Kamakau 1961:85).

More than seventy-five archaeological features make up the Keoneʻōʻio Archaeological District, and most of these are concentrated in the *kiawe*-tree-shaded strip just inland of the rocky shore. Included are both house terraces and platforms, and distinctive, rectangular stone-walled canoe sheds (*hālau*) with an opening at one end. Of particular interest is an area of a hundred or more shallow depressions artificially ground down into a pahoehoe lava shelf. These grinding depressions were probably created in the process of preparing lava abraders or files, essential tools in the manufacture of bone and shell fishhooks. Also represented in the Keoneʻōʻio complex are *heiau*, fishing shrines (*koʻa*) with upright stones, and trails.

References: Dunmore, ed. (1994:82–91); Gassner (1969:24).

23. KEʻANAE PENINSULA

During a late phase of volcanic eruptions at the summit of Haleakalā, streams of lava flowed down through Keʻanae Valley, spreading out at the coast and forming a broad, low peninsula. While the mantle of fertile soil probably developed naturally in the Koʻolau region's wet climate, Hawaiian tradition attributes the creation of this fertile plain to a local chief who was constantly at war with the neighboring people of Wailua Valley. This chief wanted to bring more land under cultivation, in order that his domain might support more people and produce more food, and hence he ordered the populace to dig and carry soil from the valley down to the flat peninsula. Thus, according to the myth, were the rich taro lands of Keʻanae created.

Keʻanae continues to be one of the last areas in the islands where taro (*kalo*) is cultivated using traditional methods, in irrigated fields (*loʻi*) whose original construc-

tion dates back to prehistoric times. The lookout along the Hāna Highway provides a superb view over the peninsula, with its reticulated grid of rectangular fields in various stages of planting and taro growth, and with the silvery irrigation ditches (*auwai*) snaking between the fields. Anthropologist E. S. C. Handy, who studied traditional Hawaiian cultivation methods in the 1930s, called Keʻanae "striking evidence of old Hawaii's ingenuity." No archaeological excavations have ever been conducted at Keʻanae, so the antiquity of human settlement and the age of the taro irrigation systems remain unknown.

References: Handy (1940:110, pl. 5a); Handy and Handy (1972:500–501); Linnekin (1985).

The fertile peninsula of Keʻanae, laid out in a rectangular grid of irrigated taro pondfields, is reputed in Hawaiian tradition to have been covered in soil carried down from the Wailua Valley.

24. *HEIAU* AT WAI'ĀNAPANAPA

The small *heiau* at Wai'ānapanapa was constructed on the rough a'a lava flow.

At Wai'ānapanapa, about two miles west of Hāna town, a delightful State park incorporates dense *hala* (*Pandanus*) forest and a wild seascape of wave-thrashed cliffs indented with tiny, black sand beaches. In Hawaiian tradition, Wai'ānapanapa is famous for its lava tube cave in which runs a freshwater stream, the scene of a bloody murder in ancient times (Beckwith 1970:381). The Hāna chief Ka'akea, a cruel and jealous man, suspected his wife Pōpō'alaea of having an affair with Ka'akea's younger brother. Pōpō'alaea and her female attendant hid in the cave, but Ka'akea found them and dashed out their brains upon the rocks. In consequence, it is said that on the night of Kū, the cave waters run red.

A short walk along the coastal trail heading east from the parking area (this trail in parts actually follows the ancient Hawaiian trail with its water-rolled stepping-stones) leads to a small *heiau* at Pa'ina Point. (The *heiau* is situated on the inland side of the old trail, just before one comes to the fence line and gate leading into private pasturelands beyond.) A small, rectangular platform about four feet high, the *heiau* is of unknown function, although it may have served as either a fishing shrine (*ko'a*) or as a Lono-class boundary *heiau*.

Reference: Beckwith (1970:381); Pearson (1970).

25. PI'ILANIHALE HEIAU

The Hāna District of Maui, extending from Ko'olau to Kaupō on the island's well-watered windward side, was once far more densely populated than at present. The fertile volcanic soils supported dryland taro, sweet potato, and breadfruit, and irrigated taro could be raised in *lo'i* fields in the narrow valleys of Kīpahulu. The large population base and abundant resources of east Maui were coveted by the ranking chiefly families, who fought to control them. According to Hawaiian oral traditions, around the year A.D. 1570, a high chief from the western side of Maui named Pi'ilani conquered the formerly independent chiefdoms of the Hāna region, uniting the entire island into one *moku* or polity. At the time of his conquest, Pi'ilani may have dedicated the great temple called Pi'ilanihale ("house of Pi'ilani"), which looms above the wild, wave-swept cliffs of Honomā'ele.

Covering nearly three acres in area, Pi'ilanihale is reputedly the largest *heiau* in the Hawaiian Islands. Architecturally, the temple consists of two separate platforms that have been connected by means of a large central terrace. The builders of Pi'ilanihale selected a broad ridge of lava rock on which to position the *heiau*, taking advantage of the natural mass in order to heighten the impressive aspect of the site. They also filled in a swale or gully some forty feet deep. The steeply terraced seaward face of the main platform—with five different terraced levels—towers above and dwarfs the viewer at its base. After passing this impressive facade, the current trail ascends the main platform along the western or coastal side. On the upper surface of the platform can be seen the foundation walls of a large rectangular enclosure (probably the *hale mana*), other low walls, various pits (some probably marking image locations), and upright stones set into the pavement. The rear of the extensive court is bounded by a superbly built stone wall seven to eight feet high.

Excavations carried out by archaeologist Michael Kolb at Pi'ilanihale Heiau in 1989–90 produced eight radiocarbon dates that provide an approximate chronology for the construction and use of this major temple. The earliest dated construction phase was from the late thirteenth to early fifteenth centuries, when the massive main terrace was built. Kolb estimated that on the order of 84,000 person-days of labor were invested in the construction of this early *heiau*. Later, during the sixteenth century and thus possibly associated with the high chief Pi'ilani, peripheral wings were added to the *heiau*, which would then have been rededicated. Another 43,000 person-days are estimated to have been required for these modifications. Final additions at the end of the eighteenth century were more modest. Thus, Pi'ilanihale, like other major *heiau* that have been archaeologically excavated (see Sites 12, 25, and 46), had a lengthy and complex architectural history that spans a period of major political and religious transformation in the Hawaiian Islands.

Note: Pi'ilanihale Heiau is contained within the grounds of the Kahanu Gardens, a branch of the Pacific Tropical Botanical Garden based at Lāwa'i, Kaua'i. Access to the *heiau* is controlled by the Garden staff, and is limited to regular visiting hours for the gardens. Contact the Pacific Tropical Botanical Garden for further information.

References: Cordy (1970); Kirch (1985:144, fig. 129); Kolb (1991).

There is probably no more impressive prehistoric stone monument in the Hawaiian Islands than the five-tiered, terraced platform of Pi'ilanihale Heiau in Hāna.

The vast scale of Pi'ilanihale Heiau is evident in this view of the main temple platform. The enclosure walls visible in the right background are seven to eight feet high.

Upright stones such as this are set into the well-paved surface of the Pi'ilanihale Heiau.

26. HISTORIC RUINS AT MOKU-LAU PENINSULA, KAUPŌ

The windswept shelf of land called Moku-lau ("many islets") after the numerous rocks jutting from the sea nearby is best known as the site of Huialoha Church, one of the Hawaiian Congregationalist "circuit" churches, constructed in 1859 with typical thick stone walls held together with lime plaster. Beyond the church and its charming graveyard surrounded by a low wall of wave-rounded lava cobbles lies a complex of historic-period ruins. Most prominent of these is a wall of rough-hewn lava blocks, pierced by a single window, and marking the site of a former schoolhouse. In such "native schools" in the mid-nineteenth century, many Hawaiians learned to read and write in their own language, using primers, Bibles, and other texts printed by the Yankee missionaries in Honolulu and at Lahainaluna. Some of these Hawaiian scholars, such as David Malo and Samuel Kamakau, later wrote important histories of their people, preserving much traditional knowledge about the ancient culture.

Seaward of the schoolhouse ruins are other features, including an early historic grave site plastered over with burnt-coral lime, and a stone-lined well. Such wells were dug by the Hawaiians who lived along coastal areas without running streams, and tapped the shallow freshwater aquifer flowing out to sea, providing water for drinking, bathing, and washing.

Although much attention is usually paid to prehistoric Hawaiian archaeological sites, the ruins at Moku-lau—along with such sites as the Russian Fort Elizabeth on Kaua'i (Site 5)—remind us that the Islands also have a rich legacy of archaeological sites dating to the historical or postcontact era. These historical sites represent many aspects of the often turbulent history of Hawai'i since the arrival of Captain James Cook in 1778.

The ruined walls of an early historic schoolhouse contrast starkly with the verdant landscape of Kaupō, Maui.

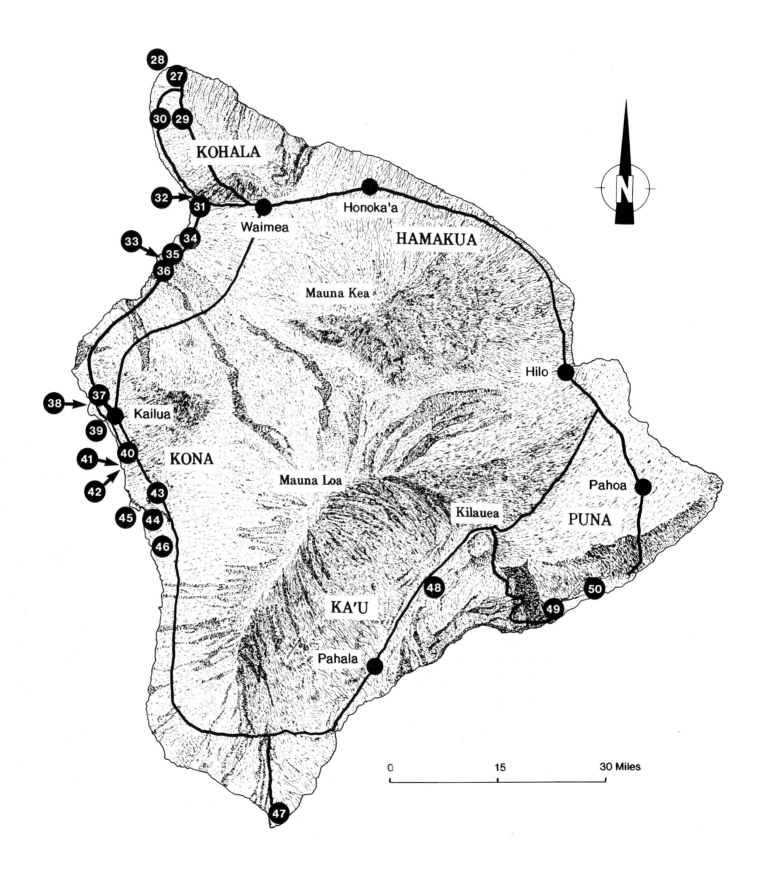

KOHALA

HAMAKUA

Honoka'a

Waimea

Mauna Kea

Hilo

KONA

Kailua

Mauna Loa

Kilauea

Pahoa

PUNA

KA'U

Pahala

N

0   15   30 Miles

HAWAI'I ISLAND

Hawai'i, popularly called the "Big Island," has a land area nearly twice that of all the other islands combined, as well as a truly remarkable range of landscapes. On no other island in the group can one go from lush windward valleys (such as Waipi'o) to barren lava fields at times only days old (on the flanks of Kīlauea) to snow-capped summits (Mauna Kea and Mauna Loa). Geologically the youngest island, Hawai'i was built up from five separate volcanoes, two of which (Mauna Loa and Kīlauea) are still active. The oldest part of the island is the northern tip, Kohala, where volcanism ceased about half a million years ago, giving sufficient time for erosion to sculpt deep valleys along the windward coast. Mauna Kea and Hualālai are technically dormant, and young enough that their slopes have been only slightly weathered. The southernmost volcanoes, Mauna Kea and Kīlauea, are highly dynamic landforms, constantly changing with each new eruption and lava flow. Kīlauea, and in particular the caldera crater of Halema'uma'u, is regarded as the abode of the volcano goddess Pele, whose cult has long been worshipped in the Puna and Ka'ū Districts of the island.

Mirroring its geological dynamism, Hawai'i Island also boasted a large, energetic, and politically aggressive population in precontact times. Oral traditions relate that for many generations the island was divided between windward and leeward, with the chiefs of each sector frequently warring with one another for political hegemony. At times certain charismatic and powerful *ali'i* would manage to bring the entire island under their rule. Among these famous chiefs were Līloa and his son 'Umi-a-Līloa, who—after conquering the rebellious district chiefs—commanded the people to carry stones to the high plateau lying between Hualālai, Mauna Loa, and Mauna Kea. There was constructed a large *heiau,* Ahu o 'Umi, as a sign of the greatness of 'Umi-a-Līloa. (The temple still stands today, although it is not readily accessible to the

public.) In the final decades of the eighteenth century, another Hawai'i Island *ali'i*—Kamehameha I—would extend the power of his island and line throughout the archipelago, establishing the Hawaiian Kingdom. Kamehameha's birthplace, and several of the great *heiau* at which he worshipped, are described below (see Sites 27, 28, 31, 39, and 50).

Traditionally, Hawai'i comprised six districts. Kohala in the north, the birthplace of Kamehameha I, included the only valleys with significant areas of irrigated taro lands, especially in Waipi'o, the seat of many great *ali'i*. Hāmākua and Hilo Districts occupied the windward regions of the island; unfortunately, the extensive development of sugarcane plantations resulted in the destruction of a significant part of the archaeological sites in these districts. The volcanically active southern slopes of Kīlauea and Mauna Loa are taken in by Puna and Ka'ū Districts. This region is rich in archaeological sites, and a number of them have been preserved and interpreted by the National Park Service (see Sites 48, 49, and 50). At the southernmost tip of the island, in Ka'ū, the Ka Lae National Historic Landmark includes many significant sites (see Site 47). The leeward, western side of the island comprises Kona and part of Kohala Districts and includes what may be the richest concentration of archaeological features in the Islands. Archaeological remains to be found here range from village sites to petroglyph concentrations, ancient trails, agricultural field systems, fishponds, and a variety of temples (see Sites 30 through 46). A number of these have been well preserved and interpreted by the National Park Service (Sites 31, 32, 37, and 46), while others are protected as State or County parks or monuments. A few sites (such as Sites 35 and 36) have been set aside by major resort developments, and are open to public visitation.

Map of Hawai'i Island.

27. MOʻOKINI HEIAU

On the windswept northern tip of Hawaiʻi Island—carrying the ancient Polynesian name of ʻUpolu (also the name of one of the Samoan Islands)—Moʻokini Heiau stands sentinel over ʻAlenuihāhā Channel, whose turbulent waters separate Hawaiʻi from Maui and the islands beyond. Tradition holds that the *heiau* was built by Pāʻao, a voyaging priest from Kahiki who introduced the practice of human sacrifice at *luakini* class temples (see Site 50). Moʻokini may be translated as "many lineages (*moʻo*)," possibly referring to the many lines of priests and chiefs who worshipped here. The *heiau* was used by Kamehameha I, whose birthplace (Site 28) lies a short distance away, along the coast to the west.

The temple displays truly monumental proportions, measuring approximately 280 feet long by 140 feet wide. Architecturally, it consists of a rectangular enclosure constructed on a slight natural elevation, so that the *heiau* is visible from some distance. The massive enclosure walls are truly impressive examples of dry-laid stonework. Pioneer archaeologist John F. G. Stokes carefully mapped and described the temple in 1906, measuring one of the least-disturbed walls as 19 feet high on the exterior, 16 feet high on the interior, and nearly 34 feet wide at the base (tapering to 6 feet wide at the top). The stones were beautifully laid, and one can only admire the skill involved in their construction. Oral tradition holds that these stones originated in the valley of Pololū, some ten miles away on the windward coast, and were passed from hand-to-hand by a continuous line of men!

Moʻokini also exhibits a number of other interesting architectural features. The raised stone altar platform, at the northern end of the massive enclosure, is rather unusual for a *luakini heiau* in having a semicircular plan and numerous small pits that reached to the underlying earth. Two smaller enclosures attach to the main *heiau* walls on the western exterior. A large, dish-shaped boulder about eight and one-half feet long, situated about fifty feet north of the temple, served as the *holehole* stone, where human sacrifices were prepared before carrying them into the enclosure to be offered up on the *lele* altar stand.

Moʻokini Heiau is a national historic landmark and State historic park; in 1992 it was officially designated part of a new Kohala Historical Sites State Monument that incorporates the Kamehameha Birthplace (Site 28) and two other *heiau* not yet readily accessible to the public. Moʻokini Heiau is managed by the nonprofit Moʻokini Luakini Foundation under the guidance of Leimomi Moʻokini Lum, a descendant of the priest Kuamoʻo Moʻokini. Mrs. Lum and the Foundation have done a superb job of protecting, maintaining, and interpreting this great monument.

References: Kamakau (1991:100); Stokes (1991:173–178, figs. 88–92).

Moʻokini Heiau in Kohala was reputedly constructed by the voyager-priest Pāʻao, and was later one of the *luakini* temples used by Kamehameha I.

An interior view in Moʻokini
Heiau, looking toward the
stone altar.

28. KOKOIKI, KAMEHAMEHA'S BIRTHPLACE

According to the nineteenth-century Hawaiian sage Samuel Kamakau, the great conquering chief Kamehameha I was born on a stormy night during the month of ʻIkuwā, in or around the year 1736:

> *He ua lokuloku no ʻIkuwā ke ʻliʻi.*
> *Ke kukuni aku la i ka lani nui;*
> *O Makaliʻi ka haoa lā wela,*
> *Hānau mai ka lani la, he ʻaoa.*

> Like the heavy rain of Ikuwa is the chief.
> Intense is the heat in the vast heavens;
> To Makaliʻi belong the intensely warm days,
> In which was born the chief, a fighter
> (Kamakau 1961:68).

Kamehameha was born of Keōua Kupuapāikalani (half-brother of the Hawaiʻi Island ruling chief Kalaniʻō-puʻu) and Kekuʻiapoiwa II. As a young man, Kamehameha was among the entourage of King Kalaniʻōpuʻu when the English explorer Captain James Cook dropped anchor in Kealakekua Bay in A.D. 1779 (see Site 45). Upon the death of Kalaniʻōpuʻu, Kamehameha was entrusted with the care of the war god Kūkāʻilimoku, while the kingdom was passed to his cousin Kiwalaʻō. Kamehameha defeated Kiwalaʻō, as well as his younger half-brother Keōua, in a series of battles for control of the island. Having gained full control of Hawaiʻi, Kamehameha I then launched his famous wars of conquest against Maui and Oʻahu, gaining full control of all islands except Kauaʻi by 1804.

Kamehameha's birth site consists of a large, stone-walled enclosure, presumably the residence of his high-ranking chiefly parents. The ground within the enclosure shows traces of waterworn gravel paving and other features. The complex lies a short distance to the west of Moʻokini Heiau, and can be approached on the same unpaved road leading to the *heiau* (passable by car if it has not been raining).

Reference: Kamakau (1961:67–68).

Chief Kamehameha I, destined to become conqueror of the archipelago and founder of a dynasty, was born in this walled residential compound on the windswept plains of Kohala.

29. KOHALA DRYLAND FIELD COMPLEX

As was the case with other early preindustrial states and civilizations, the Hawaiians had developed highly sophisticated and intensive methods of cultivation. In well-watered windward valleys (such as Hālawa, Moloka'i—see Site 17) the main emphasis was on irrigated cultivation of taro. However, on most of Hawai'i Island, as well as much of eastern Maui, streams to provide irrigation water are few or lacking, and the Hawaiians turned to intensive forms of dryland cultivation. In these agricultural field systems, the crops had to be sustained by rainfall, so that the geographical extent of the field complexes largely coincided with slightly higher altitude slopes where the combination of fertile volcanic soils and rainfall was sufficient to raise such crops as taro and sweet potatoes.

These dryland field systems were abandoned in the early years following European contact, largely as a result of the decimation of the Hawaiian population from foreign diseases. Archaeologically, however, they are still visible through the permanent modifications to the landscape made by clearing the slopes of volcanic rocks, which were heaped into long, low walls and embankments. These field walls, called *kuaiwi* ("backbone") in Hawaiian, probably had several functions, including the delineation of separate garden plots and soil retention, as well as for stone clearance. The long, rectangular spaces between the walls were used to plant a variety of crops, and the walls themselves supported windbreaks of sugarcane and *kī* plants.

Two major areas of prehistoric dryland field systems still exist on Hawai'i Island, parts of which can be viewed or visited. The Kohala Field System covers many square miles on the western flanks of the Kohala Mountains (the other area is in Kona—see Site 43). Most of this area is today covered in pasture, but in the low-angle rays of the late afternoon sun, the parallel field system walls can clearly be seen from the roadside (westward) along Highway 25 between Pu'u Kehena and Kahuā Ranch. Part of the Kohala Field System within the *ahupua'a* of Lapakahi (see Site 30) was archaeologically investigated by the University of Hawai'i in 1968–71. The archaeologists were able to determine that the vast field complex developed over a period of centuries, beginning about A.D. 1300 to 1400 and continuing up until European contact.

References: Kirch (1984:181–192); Kirch (1985:230–231); Newman (1970); Rosendahl (1994).

The grassy pasturelands of North Kohala were intensively cultivated in dryland crops in late prehistory, evidenced by the parallel lines of stone field boundaries, faintly visible in the afternoon sunlight.

Fishermen at Koaiʻe village stored their canoe hulls and outriggers in long stone-walled sheds such as this.

House sites at Koaiʻe village, first occupied around A.D. 1300.

30. KOAI'E VILLAGE SITE, LAPAKAHI *AHUPUA'A*

Around the year A.D. 1300, a group of Hawaiians—perhaps two or three related families—established a small settlement on the shores of a bay named Koai'e, along the western coastline of Kohala. The hot, arid terrain offered little in the way of agricultural potential (although the Kohala uplands some two to four miles inland provided fertile cropland for sweet potato and dryland taro; see Site 29). Rather, what attracted these people to settle at Koai'e were the rich fishing grounds offshore and the abundant shellfish, seaweed, octopus, and other edible marine resources with which the coast abounds. The Koai'e hamlet is just one of many archaeological reflections of a major episode of Hawaiian population increase that began in the thirteenth to fourteenth centuries, in what archaeologists refer to as the Expansion Period (see Introduction).

Some two centuries after Koai'e was first occupied, the settlement had grown to a substantial fishing village, bounded along its inland side by a large enclosing stone wall. The village now boasted a number of dwelling platforms and terraces, along with stone-walled canoe sheds and fishing shrines. The population of Koai'e not only trolled for fish in the offshore Pacific waters, but cultivated tuber crops in an extensive dryland field system complex some distance inland, part of the Kohala Field System (see Site 29). Habitation structures in the field system area show evidence of repeated short-term use, suggesting that the Koai'e people alternated between spending time cultivating their upland fields and living at the coast. Koai'e and the upland agricultural zone were thus integral parts of Lapakahi *ahupua'a*, a classic "pie-shaped" traditional Hawaiian land unit. Lapakahi was just one of many such *ahupua'a* closely packed together in the Kohala District.

The sophisticated pattern of land use that had developed during the Expansion Period at Lapakahi and other Kohala *ahupua'a* continued through the Proto-Historic Period, up until the arrival of Captain James Cook in 1778 and subsequent European visitors. By the time of Cook's expedition, the indigenous Hawaiian population of Kohala District may have numbered into the several tens of thousands. The devastating impact of foreign disease, however, rapidly took its toll during the first few decades following European contact; by the time of the first missionary census, the population of Kohala was reduced to 8,765 people. Koai'e Village continued to be occupied throughout the nineteenth century, probably because it was close to the developing harbor at Māhukona (which became an important port for sugar exporting after 1860). By the early twentieth century, however, Koai'e had been abandoned, its rock walls to be overtaken by exotic *kiawe* trees.

Koai'e Village and Lapakahi *ahupua'a* were the focus of a major archaeological project directed by the University of Hawai'i, primarily as a field school for the training of archaeology students, from 1968 to 1971. Their detailed surveys and excavations enabled the reconstruction of the prehistory of Koai'e. Building upon the University of Hawai'i team's research, the State of Hawaii established Lapakahi State Historical Park. Today, signed trails and interpretive programs assist the visitor in comprehending the daily life of the Hawaiian people who built and lived in this fishing village over more than six centuries.

References: Kirch (1985:177–178); Newman (1970); Tuggle and Griffin (1973).

31. PU'UKOHOLĀ AND MAILEKINI HEIAU

According to a tradition recounted by the great Hawaiian sage Kamakau, in the early years when Kamehameha I began to hatch his grand scheme of conquering all the islands of Hawai'i, he sent the chiefess Ha'alo'u on a mission to seek the advice of a famed wise man. This sayer, Kāpoūkahi, when asked by Ha'alo'u how her chief might gain control of the archipelago, responded: "'Build a great house for the god and mark out its boundaries.' Ha'alo'u asked, 'Where shall this house be?' 'At Pu'ukoholā. If he makes this house for his god, he can gain the kingdom without a scratch to his own skin.'" (Kamakau 1961:150). Kamehameha evidently took this advice to heart, and in A.D. 1790–91 he directed the construction of a massive stone temple atop a hill some four hundred feet above the sea, overlooking the natural harbor of Kawaihae. Pu'ukoholā ("hill of the whale") Heiau was probably built over the foundations of an older *heiau*—as was common practice—although no archaeological excavations have been conducted to determine this. According to Kamakau's account, Kamehameha himself labored along with his people in carrying the thousands of large stones used to build up the *heiau* platform; only his younger brother Keli'imaika'i was spared the work (thereby ceremonially maintaining the *kapu* of the chiefs).

Kamehameha dedicated Pu'ukoholā to his war god Kūkā'ilimoku, which had been entrusted to his care by the ruling chief Kalani'ōpu'u. As a *luakini heiau* consecrated to Kūkā'ilimoku and intended to assure success in war, the dedication of Pu'ukoholā required a human sacrifice, and Kamehameha had in mind the ultimate personage for this offering to his god. He dispatched two loyal chiefs, Keaweaheulu and Kamanawa, to take a message to his arch-rival Keōua in Ka'ū district, inviting the latter to Kawaihae in order to make peace. Keōua had just suffered the loss of part of his army in a terrifying

volcanic eruption at Kīlauea, a sign that the fire goddess Pele had turned against him (see Site 48). Doubtless knowing that he was going to his death, Keōua and twenty-six of his faithful followers journeyed by canoe to Kawaihae, where they were set upon by Kamehameha's warriors, and Keōua's body was laid upon the *lele* altar of Pu'ukoholā. Soon thereafter, Kamehameha led his army westward through the archipelago to a succession of victorious battles, validating the oracle of Kāpoūkahi.

Pu'ukoholā is truly an impressive monument, perched high above the bay of Kawaihae. The massive stone foundations measure 224 by 100 feet. High walls enclose the rectangular court on three sides, but the seaward side was left open, and three sets of descending terraces probably supported images. Archaeologist John F. G. Stokes, who studied the site with typical precision in 1906, observed that the "greatest care and nicety" had been used in selecting waterworn stones (*alā*) for the veneer facings.

On the slope below and seaward of Pu'ukoholā lies another substantial and reputedly older *heiau*, named Mailekini ("abundance of *maile*"). This temple site is also of rectangular plan, with a massive wall on the inland side. Stokes reported that in the early nineteenth century, it was planned to convert Mailekini into a fortress.

Both Pu'ukoholā and Mailekini temple sites are now incorporated into a national historic site under the care and protection of the National Park Service. Pu'ukoholā itself is in need of stabilization, as its walls and facings have begun to shift, and the site can presently be viewed only from the encircling trail.

References: Kamakau (1961:150, 154–155); Kirch (1985:175); Stokes (1991:164–171, figs. 78–86).

Pu'ukohalā Heiau commands a hill overlooking Kawaihae Bay.

Mailekini Heiau lies astride the slopes below the imposing Pu'ukoholā Heiau at Kawaihae.

32. JOHN YOUNG'S HOMESTEAD SITE

The final decade of the eighteenth century witnessed dramatic changes in Hawaiian society, as European and American ships began to descend on the islands and Kamehameha promulgated his ultimately successful campaign of conquest throughout the archipelago. Two British sailors, John Young and Isaac Davis, became key aides to Kamehameha in battles and in his increasing trade dealings with foreigners. Both Young and Davis arrived in the islands in 1790, Young as boatswain of the *Eleanora*, and Davis as a crew member of the *Fair American*. The *Fair American* was attacked and seized by Hawaiians in North Kona, with only Davis surviving and taken under the protection of Kamehameha. John Young was later detained by Kamehameha when the *Eleanora* visited Kealakekua Bay, for fear that he would inform the *Eleanora*'s captain about the *Fair American* disaster.

Young and Davis became trusted advisors to Kamehameha, who arranged their marriages to women of chiefly rank and gave them lands, thus converting these foreigners into haole chiefs. Young established a substantial homestead at Kawaihae, the *ahupua'a* given to him by Kamehameha I, where he frequently acted as agent between Kamehameha and visiting ships' captains. Today the site consists of the foundation walls of Young's house, built with lime plaster, and several adjacent platforms and terraces in traditional Hawaiian style. Archaeological excavations carried out for the National Park Service in 1978 yielded both native Hawaiian and imported haole artifacts, providing a glimpse into the lifestyle of this "*hapa-haole*" household.

In 1828, during a visit to Kawaihae, missionary wife Laura Fish Judd visited "old John Young, an English runaway sailor, who had been many years on the islands," and in her journal penned the only extant description of the interior of Young's house: "He lived in a dirty adobe house, adorned with old rusty muskets, swords, bayonets, and cartridge boxes. He gave us a supper of goat's meat and fried taro, served on old pewter plates, which I was unfortunate to see his servant wipe on his red flannel shirt in lieu of a napkin" (Judd 1928:36). Mrs. Judd, after "being sent up a rickety flight of stairs to sleep," evidently entertained doubts regarding the structure's stability, and around midnight descended to the "neat and comfortable" grass house of Mrs. Young, a Hawaiian chiefess of rank.

Note: Although a part of the Pu'ukoholā Heiau National Historic Site, the John Young house site (located on the *mauka* side of Route 27 from the *heiau*) is not presently marked for regular visitor access. Visitors should inquire at the park ranger's office for directions to the Young house site.

References: Rosendahl and Carter (1988).

The *'ili'ili* gravel-paved house terrace of John Young, who assisted Kamehameha I and became a *haole* chief.

33. *ALA LOA* OR MĀMALAHOA TRAIL

In prehistoric times, Hawaiians traveled along simple foot trails to reach their villages, fields, and favored fishing spots. Where these trails had to cross rough terrain, such as jagged a'a lava that can lacerate a person's foot, stepping-stones of smooth, wave-rolled cobbles were often carefully positioned. Fist-sized pieces of sun-bleached, white coral were sometimes placed along a trail to reflect moonlight and permit the traveler to pass at night.

An American, Richard J. Cleveland, introduced the first horses to Hawai'i in 1803, although they were still rare and mostly the property of ranking chiefs until the late 1820s. The old Hawaiian trails were unsuited to horses and as the popularity of horseback travel increased after 1820, new routes needed to be constructed. Kuakini (Governor of Hawai'i, 1819–44), a high chief who had acquired horses (he lent one to the missionary wife Lucy G. Thurston in 1825), undertook a program of road building using prison labor. Clusters of small stone shelters—crudely constructed and C-shaped—situated near the trails mark the encampments of the prisoner work gangs.

An excellent example of Kuakini's trail-building scheme of the 1820s and 30s can be seen at 'Anaeho'omalu. The trail, about five feet wide and lined on both sides with low curbstones, passes directly through the 'Anaeho'omalu petroglyph field (see Site 35). Unlike the sinuous prehistoric Hawaiian trails, this new road was constructed in a straight line, with causeways and ramps provided where it crossed gaps or fissures in the rugged lava fields.

References: Apple (1965:33–34); Kirch (1985:270).

The Māmalahoa Trail, built with prisoner labor in the early nineteenth century, crosses the barren pahoehoe lava flats at 'Anaeho'omalu.

34. PUAKŌ ARCHAEOLOGICAL DISTRICT

The island of Hawai'i boasts no less than 70 out of approximately 135 documented petroglyph sites in the archipelago (Cox with Stasack 1970:7). A large number of these Hawai'i Island rock-art sites (which include a total of about 22,600 individual glyph units) are found in the leeward parts of the island, especially in Kohala, Kona, and Ka'ū Districts. One of the most famous of these petroglyph concentrations, exhibiting some 3,000 glyph units along a portion of the old Ka'eo Trail, lies within the Puakō Archaeological District. (The Puakō petroglyph fields, which are maintained as a historic preserve with public access, may be approached from the park at the northern end of Kanikū Drive, within the Mauna Lani Resort complex.)

The Puakō petroglyphs were pecked or incised into the billowy surface of a pahoehoe lava flow, which is typical of the majority of petroglyphs on the island of Hawai'i. Pahoehoe lava, which contains a high volume of gasses and thus flows rapidly, forms low mounds with smooth or ropy surfaces when it cools.

> The surface tends to harden into a glaze that resists erosion. When broken by the petroglyph maker, the exposed granular interior contrasts with the undisturbed surface. Petroglyphs on these surfaces tend to show up very well, as they were easily made to an inch or so in depth. However, some tend to erode by the crumbling of the sharp edge of the glaze, which disrupts the clarity of the images (Cox with Stasack 1970:9–10).

The Puakō petroglyphs display a remarkable variety of motifs, including numerous variants of human or anthropomorphic figures, representations of animals, and geometric figures (concentric circles, dots, lines) whose intended meaning is problematic to archaeological interpretation. The human figures occur singly, or in groups that may represent family units; in some cases, the sex of the figures is indicated, and birthing scenes are also depicted (see Cox with Stasack 1970:17, 50, figs. 20, 65, 67, 72). Given the predominance of such family grouping and birthing scenes, it is conceivable that the Puakō complex had a particular function or significance relating to birth.

One of the most remarkable sets of figures, clearly executed as a complete composition, features a line of twenty-nine stick figures "marching" in single file, with three larger figures standing off to the left of the column. To the right is a vastly larger figure, possibly representing the *akua loa* or "long god" of the annual *makahiki* procession. Cox and Stasack (1970:34) argue that the whole composition "brings to mind a picture of the *makahiki* procession moving along a trail accompanied by the priests of Lono." Alternately, it is plausible to interpret this scene as a party of warriors—commanded by their chief—heading to or from some battle. Animal motifs present at Puakō include dogs, chickens, and sea turtles.

References: Cox with Stasack (1970:85); Kirch (1985:170, 271).

Puakō Archaeological District incorporates one of the most extensive petroglyph fields in the Islands.

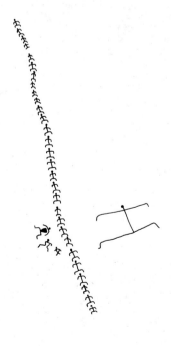

Petroglyphs at Puakō (Site 34), after Cox and Stasack (1970).

35. KALĀHUIPUA'A

The leeward, coastal region of South Kohala District is among the most arid regions of the Hawaiian Islands. The pahoehoe and a'a lava flows—radiating intense heat during midday—appear to stretch away endlessly toward distant Mauna Kea. Here and there along this coast, however, are a few shallow bays rimmed with brackish-water fishponds and coconut groves: oases that drew native Hawaiians to fish and reside seasonally. One such pocket of water and life amid the lava desert is at Kalāhuipua'a, along the northern edge of the great Kanikū a'a lava flow.

The attraction at Kalāhuipua'a was surely the cluster of fresh and brackish-water pools and ponds that fill natural basins and fissures in the older pahoehoe lava terrain adjacent to the massive and incredibly jagged Kanikū flow. Archaeological and geological evidence reveals that the island of Hawai'i is gradually sinking into the surrounding Pacific Ocean floor at the rate of about eight inches every hundred years. As the shoreline subsided, some of the natural depressions in the lava began to fill with underground streams of fresh water flowing seaward, and with salt water seeping in through the porous rocks. The brackish-water ponds formed by these processes—now physically closed to the sea—are called *anchialine* ponds. The anchialine ponds are the habitat

of a small, red shrimp (*ōpae'ula*) endemic to Hawai'i. The larger ponds at Kalāhuipua'a are partly open to the sea, and the Hawaiians transformed them into fishponds for mullet (*'ama'ama*) and milkfish (*awa*) by constructing stone walls across the open gaps, and installing *mākāhā* gates (see Site 16, Moloka'i Fishponds). The fresh water flowing through the porous lava near the ponds also permits coconut palms (*niu*), *milo* trees (prized for their wood), and such useful plants as *noni* (used for medicine) and *hala* (for weaving mats) to grow thickly around the pond margins.

Archaeological exploration of Kalāhuipua'a in the 1970s (Kirch 1979) revealed the presence of some 212 sites clustered in a concentric zone around the lush ponds. Some of these sites were shelter caves formed by lava tubes and gas pockets in the pahoehoe, exposed by partial collapse. Such caves provided cool shade and shelter from the dry winds, and were the main dwelling places of the prehistoric Hawaiians who visited and fished at Kalāhuipua'a. Excavations in the midden deposits forming the floors of several shelter caves yielded fishhooks carved of bone and shell, along with abrading tools of coral and scoria, basalt adzes, and other tools and implements. These sites were used for a period of about

Fishponds at Kalāhuipua'a, filling natural depressions in the pahoehoe lava, provided a resource that attracted people to the arid South Kohala coast as early as A.D. 1200.

five hundred years, beginning around A.D. 1200. In one storage cave, a cache of sixteen large wooden fishhooks had been left by an ancient fisherman, possibly an expert in the art of catching large jacks (*ulua*) or sharks (*manō*). Outside the caves can be found other kinds of sites, such as simple C-shaped windbreak walls, petroglyphs pecked or incised into the flat lava surface, and sets of shallow, basin-shaped depressions ground into the lava as a result of sharpening and shaping the scoria abraders used in fishhook making.

Other kinds of sites are found on the jagged surface of the great Kanikū lava flow, near the shoreline. The coastal trail still follows the old Hawaiian trail for the most part, which is paved in places with water-rolled stepping-stones carried up from the boulder beaches. At Waʻawaʻa Point, a small group of stone structures marks the site of a fisherman's household. Some distance inland, the Ala Loa—the so-called King's Highway—crosses the Kanikū flow in a straight path between Kalāhuipuaʻa and ʻAnaehoʻomalu. This stone-lined trail (see Site 33, Māmalahoa Trail) was constructed in the 1820s and 30s using prison labor, under the direction of Kuakini, Governor of Hawaiʻi from 1819 to 1844.

Note: Two historic preserves at Kalāhuipuaʻa are maintained by the Mauna Lani Resort. The well-signed main preserve (with petroglyphs, shelter caves, and abrading depressions) can be approached via the public park (with parking and restrooms) off Mauna Lani Drive, while the smaller preserve at Waʻawaʻa Point can only be accessed via the Ala Kahakai coastal trail. Visitors are advised to check with Mauna Lani Resort (808-885-6677).

Reference: Kirch (1979).

Natural lava tubes at Kalāhuipuaʻa provided cool shelter from the sun and wind. Archaeological excavations in midden deposits within these shelters reveal a long history of occupation by Hawaiian fishermen and their households.

36. PETROGLYPHS AT ʻANAEHOʻOMALU

Heading south from Kalāhuipuaʻa and crossing the broad expanse of the Kanikū lava flow, one reaches another fishpond oasis: the bay of ʻAnaehoʻomalu with its gently curving arc of salt-and-pepper-colored sand. As at Kalāhuipuaʻa, the fishpond at ʻAnaehoʻomalu was surrounded by a dense zone of archaeological sites, many of which were destroyed when the present hotel was constructed in the 1970s. These included open habitation sites, shelter caves, and burial caves. Farther inland, on the barren pahoehoe lava adjacent to the Māmalahoa Trail (see Site 33), a large petroglyph site is accessible on foot from a footpath leading through the hotel's golf course.

The large ʻAnaehoʻomalu petroglyph field is clearly associated with the Māmalahoa trail, which existed first as a sinuous footpath worn into the lava, and later as a historic-period trail modified for horse travel. The various images carved into the rock along the trail side were presumably made by travelers who may have stopped here to rest. In 1823, the English missionary William Ellis made a tour of Hawaiʻi Island, and provided the first written account of petroglyphs: "We frequently saw a number of straight lines, semicircles, or concentric rings, with some rude imitations of the human figure, cut or carved in the compact rocks of lava" (Ellis 1963:334). Ellis inquired of his Hawaiian guides the meaning of these symbols, and was told that "they had been made by former travelers . . . to inform his successors that he has been there." The missionary went on to decode the meaning of some of the frequently occurring geometric motifs:

> When there were a number of concentric circles with a dot or mark in the centre, the dot signified a man, and the number of rings denoted the number in the party who had circumambulated the island.

When there was a ring, and a number of marks, it denoted the same; the number of marks shewing [sic] how many the party consisted; and the ring, that they had traveled completely round the island; but when there was only a semicircle, it denoted that they had returned after reaching the place where it was made (Ellis 1963:334).

The carving of petroglyphs at ʻAnaehoʻomalu evidently spanned both the prehistoric and early historic periods. Most of the glyphs are of traditional forms (such as concentric circles and human figures), but some include obviously post–European-contact images. One of the most famous of these images is a horse and rider scene (see Cox with Stasack 1970:16, fig. 18). There are also names carved into the lava surface in large capital-block letters, probably dating to the years following the issuance of the first Hawaiian language texts by the Protestant missionaries. In the 1820s a great frenzy of literacy swept the islands, with the missionaries reporting that thousands of "scholars" were engaged in studies, learning to read and write.

At many petroglyph sites, evidence of continued carving over a long period is provided by complex overlapping of motifs. One such highly complex arrangement at ʻAnaehoʻomalu was analyzed by Cox and Stasack (1970: 48–51, figs. 70–71). The scene began with a large human figure, to which various circles and dots were added. Subsequently, an arc over the head (possibly representing a rainbow), parallel lines, "footprints," and other motifs were added until the design became highly complex.

References: Barrera (1971); Cox with Stasack (1970:85); Kirch (1985:169, fig. 150).

Petroglyph motifs pecked into the pahoehoe lava at 'Anaeho'omalu include a "crab-claw" sail in the foreground, and various human figures.

At 'Anaeho'omalu, the tread of countless feet have worn the ancient prehistoric trail smooth. Petroglyphs surround the trail on both sides.

37. KALOKO FISHPOND

The sun-baked lava fields stretching north of Kailua in Kona were known collectively to the Hawaiians as Kekaha, an *ʻāina maloʻo* or parched land. Despite their aridity, these lands were prized by the chiefs because of the fishponds dotting the coastline. During the Great Mahele or division of lands between King Kamehameha III and his ranking chiefs in 1848, the *ahupuaʻa* of Kaloko with its extensive walled fishpond was reserved as the personal estate of Lot Kamehameha (grandson of Kamehameha I and later to become Kamehameha V). King Kauikeaouli (Kamehameha III) reserved the nearby *ahupuaʻa* of Haleʻōhiʻu and Puʻu Waʻawaʻa, also harboring large ponds. Indeed, the Kamehameha family is even more intimately associated with Kaloko, for according to some authorities, it was in a burial cave near the fishpond that Kameʻeiamoku and Hoapili hid the bones of the great conqueror, Kamehameha I, after his death at Kailua in 1819 (Kamakau 1964:41). Dorothy Barrère (1975) recounts in detail the fascinating but unresolved saga of the search for Kamehameha's final resting place, of which "the morning star alone knows."

In 1978, the Kaloko–Honokōhau National Historical Park was established by act of Congress, ensuring the preservation not only of Kaloko and ʻAimakapā fishponds, but of a major complex of archaeological features surrounding these features. An extensive archaeological study of this area was carried out by Ross Cordy and his colleagues in 1970–71, revealing several hundred stone structures and features. Radiocarbon dates from their excavations indicate that initial Hawaiian use of the area began as early as A.D. 1000.

The fishpond at Kaloko differs from those typically seen on other islands, as along the southern shore of Molokaʻi (see Site 16), in that it was constructed by walling off a natural indentation in the rocky shoreline, rather than by extending a wall out from shore. This method reflects the absence of a shallow reef flat along the geologically youthful Hawaiʻi Island coast.

References: Barrère (1975); Cordy et al. (1991); Kelly (1971).

In the early morning calm, the still waters of Kaloko Fishpond reflect the exotic *kiawe* trees rimming the far shore.

38. MAKA'ŌPI'O HEIAU AT HONOKŌHAU

As forbidding as the coastal parts of North Kona District might appear to the first-time visitor—with their vast empty stretches of jagged a'a and ropy pahoehoe lava—the coastline here is actually a dense zone of archaeological sites. For the Hawaiian populace, the attraction was the rich fishing grounds offshore, as well as the natural anchialine fishponds (see Site 35, Kalāhuipua'a). In North Kona, the adjacent *ahupua'a* of Kaloko (see Site 37), Honokōhau, and Kealakehe contain a virtually continuous archaeological site complex along their coastal sectors. According to archaeologists K. P. Emory and L. J. Soehren, these *ahupua'a* contain more than fifty ancient house sites, four *heiau*, and a number of fishponds. These lands were among the private reserves of the Kamehameha line of ruling chiefs. Much of this area lies within the boundaries of the Kaloko–Honokōhau National Historical Park, although at the time of this writing most of these sites have not yet been opened for visitation.

One particularly interesting *heiau* site, however, is readily accessible to the public; indeed, many beachgoers pass by it daily on their way to 'Alula Bay, immediately south of the Honokōhau Boat Harbor. (Follow the road along the south side of the harbor all the way to the shore and park in the informal lot; the site is just off the trail to the beach.) This is Maka'ōpi'o Heiau, a rectangular stone platform about 34 by 54 feet in size, constructed over a natural depression in the pahoehoe lava amidst several brackish-water ponds. The name Maka'ōpi'o ("eye of the child") was given by an elderly Hawaiian authority, Naluahine, when interviewed in 1957. The temple was supposedly a fishing *heiau*, or *ko'a*.

What makes the site unusual are the two massive, rectangular stone slabs set upright and placed approximately equidistant in the seaward (western) face of the stone platform. Each stone slab measures about four feet wide by seven feet high, and is about a foot thick. They appear to have been cut and dressed, although subsequent weathering from high surf has obscured any traces of working. Naluahine stated that these slabs were *kū'ula* (fish gods), and that they had been brought here from Kailua.

References: Emory and Soehren (1971:9–11, fig. 5); Kirch (1985:167, fig. 148).

Two massive basalt slabs rise from the seaward face of Maka'ōpi'o Heiau at Honokōhau.

39. AHU'ENA HEIAU

In August of 1812, Kamehameha I—who had resided on O'ahu since his successful conquest and amalgamation of the Kingdom in 1804—left Honolulu with his entourage for his ancestral island of Hawai'i. He made his home at the small cove of Kamakahonu ("eye of the turtle"), at the edge of Kailua Bay, and remained there until his death seven years later. After his wars of conquest, during which he worshipped his war god Kūkā'ilimoku and built or rededicated several *luakini heiau* (see Sites 31 and 50), Kamehameha quietly put aside the worship of Kū and focused on the cult of Lono, god of agriculture and prosperity. Traditionally, Lono was worshipped during the *makahiki*—the new year's harvest ceremonial—when the Lono priests would make a right-hand circuit of the island, collecting tribute at each *ahupua'a*.

At Kamakahonu, Kamehameha established a Hale o Lono ("house of Lono") *heiau* to hold the collection of gods he had seized from his vanquished foes, and in which to hold his ritual observances. The *heiau*, Ahu'ena ("red-hot altar"), was built upon the foundation of an older temple, probably dating to the time of Hawai'i Island chief Līloa. Fortunately, a number of accounts both by native Hawaiians and by visiting Europeans offer a good description of Ahu'ena Heiau and the role it played in the daily life of Kamehameha's household. Also, the French artist Louis Choris made a sketch of the temple, its thatched houses, and its god images in 1816. Choris' sketch provides one of the few firsthand depictions of a Hawaiian religious site while in use, prior to the overthrow of the old religious order after Kamehameha's death in 1819.

The Hawaiian scholar John Papa 'I'i, who served with the court of Kamehameha during his youth and later authored his memoirs of this period ('I'i:1959), described Ahu'ena during the years that Kamehameha worshipped there:

> Ahuena house, which was a heiau, was enclosed with a fence of lama wood and within this fence, toward the front on the west and facing inland, there was an anu'u tower. A row of images stood along its front, as befitted a Hale o Lono. Images stood at the northwest corner of the house, with a stone pavement in front of them that extended as far as the western gate and as far as the fence east of the house. On the west side of the outer entrance was a large image named Koleamoku, on whose helmet perched the figure of a plover (1959:123).

During Kamehameha's last years, his council met regularly within Ahu'ena to discuss the affairs of state, and also to give instruction to his son Liholiho in history and ways of the great chiefs, that he might rule wisely after his father's death.

Kamakahonu is today part of the grounds of the King Kamehameha Hotel in Kailua, Kona, and Ahu'ena Heiau was restored in the late 1970s as part of a hotel refurbishing. The stone foundations were excavated and rebuilt under archaeological supervision, and the wooden and thatched superstructures, as well as the god images, were recreated primarily on the basis of the 1816 sketch by Louis Choris. This site provides an excellent impression of how a typical Hale o Lono temple must have looked during use.

References: Barrère (1975:7–9); 'I'i (1959:123–124); Kirch (1985:166, fig. 147); Stokes (1991:43–47, fig. 7).

Ahuʻena Heiau, recon-
structed to conform to an
early historic drawing by
Choris, occupies a stone
platform built out over the
water at Kamakahonu, the
residence of Kamehameha I.

"Temple du Roi dans la baie
Tiritatea." Drawing by Louis
Choris of Ahuʻena Heiau in
1822. (Courtesy of the
Bishop Museum)

40. KUʻEMANU HEIAU

Ancient Hawaiians invented the sport of surfing on wooden boards (*heʻe nalu*), a sport which has now become international. In precontact times, there were two kinds of surfboard, a short form (about six to nine feet long) called *alaia*, and a longer one called *olo* that measured as much as fifteen feet (Buck 1957:384–386). Surfing was a sport practiced primarily by chiefs.

Kahaluʻu Bay is a favored surfing spot when the southern swells surge into the bay, and situated on the northern point is the only documented surfing *heiau* in the Islands. Kuʻemanu Heiau lies immediately adjacent to Aliʻi Drive, and is protected as a State historic site. Pioneer archaeologist John F. G. Stokes, who carried out a survey of Hawaiʻi Island *heiau* in 1906, was told by the local Hawaiians that Kuʻemanu "was a *heiau* for surf-riding, where they could pray for good surfing weather and consequently good sport. The terraces were excellent points of vantage from which to watch the sport, and the pool convenient for removing the salt on the return" (1991:70).

Architecturally, Kuʻemanu Heiau has a roughly rectangular main terrace, with a low platform paved in fine water-rolled gravel. On the north side of the terrace are two walled enclosures and a small pit that Stokes reported to have been a *luapaʻū*—a depository for sacrificial offerings. South of the main terrace lies the freshwater bathing pool, where surfing contestants reputedly rinsed off the salt water, and a small well for drinking water.

Reference: Stokes (1991:67–70, fig. 20).

The main platform of Kuʻemanu Heiau affords an unimpeded view of Kahaluʻu Bay, a favorite surfing spot in ancient times, as it is today.

The inner stacked-stone facing of Kuʻemanu Heiau, a temple dedicated to the chiefly sport of surf-riding.

41. HĀPAIALIʻI HEIAU, KAHALUʻU

Kona District contains an amazing array of *heiau* sites, most situated adjacent to the coastline. Many of these have been destroyed or are not readily accessible, but two prominent sites can be approached through the main drive and grounds of the Keauhou Beach Hotel. Hāpaialiʻi ("pregnant chiefess") Heiau was constructed on a dramatic location, atop a pahoehoe lava flat at the water's edge, surrounded by tide pools. Architecturally, the *heiau* consists only of a single rectangular platform, surmounted by a low three-sided enclosure and small platform in the center. The dry stone masonry techniques used in the main platform, however, are remarkable both in the size and regularity of the large lava blocks and in the visually appealing nature of the facade.

Little information has been preserved about the temple or those who constructed and used it. Pioneering archaeologist John F. G. Stokes, who mapped the site in 1906, was told that the *heiau* had been built by a Maui *kahuna* named Maʻa. T. G. Thrum, however, was given the contradictory information that Hāpaialiʻi Heiau had been constructed by Kamehameha in about A.D. 1782, after he defeated Kiwalaʻō at the battle of Mokuʻōhai. Such discrepancies are not uncommon in Hawaiian archaeology, and sadly remind us of how much knowledge concerning ancient sites has been lost in the past two hundred years.

Reference: Stokes (1991:71–74, figs. 21–23).

Hāpaialiʻi Heiau was built of massive pahoehoe lava slabs laid out over the tidal flat.

The partially collapsed seawall of Ke'ekū Heiau reveals construction details.

42. KE'EKŪ HEIAU, KAHALU'U

Situated only about 150 feet southwest of Hāpaiali'i Heiau, across the tide-pool-dotted pahoehoe flat, lies Ke'ekū Heiau. Although it has suffered much damage along its outer walls from storm surf over the centuries, this is a much more massive and imposing structure than its neighbor. Ke'ekū Heiau forms an approximate rectangle of massive stone walls reaching heights of eleven feet, in places more than thirty feet wide. There is a narrow entrance from the beach on the south, while the interior floor is largely covered in sand. The site has not been well maintained in recent years, and the interior is overgrown with shrubs. The adjacent Lagoon Hotel was abandoned, its owners evidently in bankruptcy at the time we photographed it, an all-too-poignant symbol of the rampant overdevelopment of Hawai'i in the 1970s and 1980s.

Archaeologist John F. G. Stokes was able to obtain considerably more information in 1906 about Ke'ekū Heiau than its neighbor Hāpaiali'i. Apparently Ke'ekū served not only as a *luakini* class *heiau* in which human sacrifices were offered, but also as a *pu'uhonua* or place of refuge for *kapu* breakers. Stokes was told that the temple had been built by the famous chief Lonoikama-kahiki who, after defeating the Maui king Kamalālāwalu, had offered up his foe's body on the *lele* altar of Ke'ekū. The famous nineteenth-century Hawaiian scholar Samuel Kamakau mentions this temple under the longer name Kama-i-ke'ekū, and remarks that Kamehameha included it as one of the many *heiau* he established for human sacrifice (1961:180).

References: Emory, McCoy, and Barrère (1971:16–19, figs. 4-6); Stokes (1991:74–79, figs. 24–30).

43. KONA FIELD SYSTEM (AMY GREENWELL ETHNOBOTANICAL GARDEN)

On the western side of Hawai'i Island, where the geologically youthful lava slopes have not yet been significantly eroded and where streams are generally lacking, the Hawaiians developed sophisticated methods of dryland agriculture. One vast prehistoric dryland field system in the Kohala District was described earlier (see Site 29). A second dryland agricultural complex was focused on the Kona area, in the uplands overlooking the coast from Kailua south to Kealakekua and beyond. This vast Kona Field System may have covered as much as sixty square miles at the time of Captain James Cook's visit in A.D. 1779, when the Hawaiian population of the island numbered in the hundreds of thousands.

Much of the Kona Field System has subsequently been destroyed or altered through two centuries of ranching, cash-crop cultivation (especially for coffee), and other land developments. Fortunately, however, a small sample of the prehistoric agricultural field walls and other gardening features has been preserved at the Amy Greenwell Ethnobotanical Garden in the town of Captain Cook, above Kealakekua. The grounds of the Garden, an ethnobotanical research station run by the Bishop Museum, include several of the ancient *kuaiwi* walls and intervening garden plots (*kīhāpai*). Unlike the dryland field walls in Kohala, which run across the slope of the land, the Kona walls run with the slope. The Garden staff have replanted the area in various native Hawaiian plants and cultigens used by the Hawaiian gardeners, making this a unique facility for interpreting and understanding traditional horticulture and ethnoecology.

The intensively cultivated agricultural fields on the slopes above Kealakekua Bay—in the vicinity of the Greenwell Ethnobotanical Garden—were well described in A.D. 1793 by Archibald Menzies, the naturalist assigned to Captain George Vancouver's expedition. Having already passed through the lower altitude zone dominated by large breadfruit trees ('ulu, *Artocarpus altilis*), Menzies entered "more and more fertile" countryside, "in a high state of cultivation":

> For several miles round us there was not a spot that would admit of it but what was with great labor and industry cleared of the loose stones and planted with esculent roots or some useful vegetables or other. In clearing the ground, the stones are heaped up in ridges between the little fields and planted on each side, either with a row of sugar cane or the sweet root of these islands, where they afterwards continue to grow in a wild state, so that even these stony, uncultivated banks are by this means made useful to the proprietors, as well as ornamental to the fields they intersect (Menzies 1920:75–76).

The "sweet root" referred to by Menzies was the *kī* plant (*Cordyline terminalis*), well known for its long leaves used to wrap *laulau* food bundles and for other functions, and for its root, which when baked in an earth oven becomes quite sweet and edible. These *kī* plants have continued to grow on the stone *kuaiwi* walls at the Greenwell Garden, and can be admired by visitors to the site today.

The main crops produced in the Kona Field System, however, were not the *kī* or sugarcane, which served mainly as windbreaks and supplemental crops. Rather, as Menzies and other early visitors to the area described,

Kī plants, with edible roots and leaves used to wrap foods for baking, grow wild on the *kuaiwi* walls at the Greenwell Ethnobotanical Garden. These *kī* plants have evidently survived since the time of indigenous Hawaiian cultivation.

Stone walls called *kuaiwi*, such as this example at the Greenwell Ethnobotanical Garden, separated intensively cultivated fields in the Kona uplands.

the Hawaiian farmers concentrated on growing dryland taro (*kalo, Colocasia esculenta*), sweet potato (*'uala, Ipomoea batatas*), and paper mulberry (*wauke, Broussonetia papyrifera*). The taro and sweet potato, which thrived in the fertile volcanic soils of the Kona uplands, provided the main starch staples upon which the densely settled Hawaiian population of western Hawai'i Island depended for sustenance. The *wauke* shrubs, on the other hand, yielded bark that was processed and beaten to create a variety of textures and kinds of *kapa* (tapa or bark cloth) for loincloths, skirts, bed sheets, and other domestic uses.

Although the Kona soils are fertile, they easily become dried out, and the Hawaiians had to develop special horticultural techniques and practices in order to maintain high yields. Menzies described how the gardeners he saw covered their fields "with a thick layer of hay, made from long, coarse grass or the tops of sugar cane, which continually preserves a certain degree of moisture in the soil that would otherwise be parched up by the

scorching heat of the solar rays" (1920:75–76). Within the Greenwell Garden complex are found many Hawaiian gardening features, such as stone-faced terraces and small, circular planting mounds of heaped-up stones.

Archaeological investigations in the Greenwell Garden complex that I carried out in the late 1970s provided additional details on the ancient Hawaiian cultivation methods and on the chronology of the Kona Field System. Radiocarbon dates on charcoal excavated from beneath the *kuaiwi* walls and other features indicate that the field system was in use by the later Expansion Period and on into the Proto-Historic Period.

Note: Prior to scheduling a visit to the Amy Greenwell Ethnobotanical Garden, please call the office (808-323-3318) to determine public hours and the availability of guided tours.

References: Kelly (1983); Kirch (1985:225–230, fig. 198); Menzies (1920:75–76); Newman (1970).

Ferns grow luxuriantly in the shade of the massive retaining wall of Hikiau Heiau.

On this ʻiliʻili-paved terrace at Hikiau Heiau, Captain James Cook was installed as the returning god Lono on January 18, 1779.

"An Offering before Captain Cook in the Sandwich Islands." Original watercolor by John Webber, artist on Cook's third voyage, depicts the famous navigator receiving an offering of baked pig at Hikiau Heiau. (Courtesy of the Bishop Museum)

44. HIKIAU HEIAU

In the early evening of January 17th, 1779—a Sunday—Lt. William Bligh returned to H.M.S. *Resolution* after a scouting foray in the ship's boat. Bligh reported to Captain James Cook that he had found a "tolerable shelterd bay, a good beach to land & behind it a pond of indifferent water." The bay was named Kealakekua ("pathway of the god"), in the Kona District (Lt. King, in Beaglehole 1967:502). After weeks of ceaseless sailing, Cook and his crew were eager to drop anchor for resupply and refreshment. The *Resolution* and her sister ship *Discovery* entered the bay on Monday morning, surrounded by such a throng of canoes as the English explorers had never before encountered on their Pacific voyages. Lt. King estimated fifteen hundred canoes; the *Discovery* "had such a number of people hanging on one side that she heal'd considerably" (Beaglehole 1967:504).

Cook and his officers landed on the rocky beach, where they were "receiv'd by 3 or 4 men who held wands tipt with dogs hair, & who kept repeating a sentence, wherein the word Erono [Lono] was always mention'd" (Lt. King, in Beaglehole 1967:504). Although the English navigators were ignorant of this, Kealakekua Bay was the beginning and ending point for the annual circuit of the island made by the Lono priests during the *makahiki* harvest season. Captain Cook, it would appear, was being received as the manifestation or reincarnation of Lonoikamakahiki, the god-chief who returned ritually each year to bring the *kona* rains and replenish the land. The English had already noticed a temple (Cook called it a *"morai"* after the Tahitian word) situated at the southern end of the bay, and to this "pile of stones" they were now conducted by the Hawaiians.

What ensued on the great stone *heiau* platform of Hikiau was the ceremony of *hānaipū*, the annual homage performed to the temple image of Lono, with one signal distinction: Cook himself was treated as the Lono god would normally be, evidence that—according to anthropologist Marshall Sahlins—the Captain was being installed as Lono incarnate. Cook was made to sit between two wooden images with his arms held outstretched, while the priests chanted their prayers and the crowd repeated the chorus of "O Lono." The expedition artist, John Webber, sketched the scene that was later engraved for the official Admiralty account of the voyage. Some days after Cook's installation as Lono, one of the ship's gunners—William Watman by name—passed away after a long illness, and at the Hawaiian chiefs' request was buried in the Hikiau Heiau platform.

The stone foundations of Hikiau Heiau lie at Nāpōʻopoʻo, at the end of the road leading to Kealakekua Bay. Extensive architectural modifications to the *heiau*, both during the time of Kamehameha I and after, have changed the shape and details of the stone foundation from that of Cook's time. Nonetheless, the great rectangular platform of stacked lava rocks remains intact, with an impressive northern facing sixteen feet high. From this platform one can look down on the sacred freshwater pool just north of the temple, which was surrounded by the houses of the priests. The surface of the Hikiau platform is finely paved with *ʻiliʻili* pebbles, and toward the eastern end of the platform is a stone-walled enclosure that may have supported the thatched structure depicted in John Webber's sketch. From Lt. King's journal, it seems clear that Hikiau functioned as a *luakini heiau*, and that the main god image was that of Kū, deity of war and conquest.

References: Beaglehole (1967:504–507; 517, Pl. 55); Kirch (1985:164–166); Sahlins (1981:20–22); Stokes (1991:98–102, figs. 44–49).

45. KA'AWALOA VILLAGE SITE

The great bay of Kealakekua ("path of the god")—which provided Captain Cook's ships a fair anchorage—lies within the core of Kona District, a densely populated region during the Expansion and Proto-Historic Periods. Dramatic cliffs rising abruptly from the sea along the northern shore of the bay—the Pali Kapu o Keōua, famed for its burial caves—separate the village of Nāpō'opo'o (location of Hikiau Heiau, Site 44) from Ka'awaloa. Situated on a level flat of land projecting into the sea—created by a lava flow from Mauna Loa—Ka'awaloa was a dwelling place of chiefs (the name translates as "the distant kava," referring to runners who brought the narcotic plant to the chiefs from as far away as Waipi'o Valley).

At the time of Captain Cook's visit, Ka'awaloa was the royal seat of the Hawai'i Island paramount chief, Kalani'ōpu'u, by then an old man who had ruled the island for many years. Cook's relations with Kalani'ōpu'u had been peaceable during the weeks that H.M.S. *Discovery* and *Resolution* were anchored in Kealakekua Bay, even though the Hawaiians had begun to inquire with increasing frequency as to when the British would take their leave. Cook sailed his ships out of Kealakekua on February 4, but ran into unexpectedly strong winds off North

Kohala—winds that sprung the *Resolution*'s foremast and forced a return to the shelter of Kealakekua Bay. In marked contrast to the celebratory crowds that had greeted him as "Lono" in January, Cook now found a nearly deserted bay and a sullen demeanor on the part of the few Hawaiians willing to trade with the ships. As anthropologist Marshall Sahlins explains, "Cook was now *hors catégorie*. . . . The abrupt reappearance of the ships was a contradiction to all that had gone before" (1981:22–23).

The theft of a valuable ship's boat was a provocation that Cook could not ignore, and on Sunday morning, February 14, 1779, the Captain—escorted by a party of marines—landed at Ka'awaloa with the intention of taking hostage the ruling chief Kalani'ōpu'u. To the Hawaiians, this action was a direct challenge by Lono to the rule of the king. Awakened at his house in Ka'awaloa Village, Kalani'ōpu'u began to walk with Cook down the stone-walled path to the seaside, when he was stopped by his favored wife Kāneikapōlei and two chiefs. They "told him such stories of the death of kings as to force him to sit upon the ground" (Sahlins 1985:107), where he now sat "dejected and frightened." Meanwhile, the word of

"Death of Captain James Cook, February 14, 1779, Kealakekua Bay." This rendition of Cook's death is by John Webber, artist on the third voyage. (Courtesy of the Bishop Museum)

Captain James Cook's ships *Resolution* and *Discovery* dropped anchor in Kealakekua Bay, under the shadow of the Pali Kapu o Keōua, in January 1779.

The white obelisk, surrounded by a fence made of naval cannon and ball, was erected by the British government near the spot where Captain Cook fell on February 14, 1779.

Cook's attempt to take the king hostage had spread, and a crowd of armed Hawaiians—numbering perhaps to three thousand—gathered to defend their ruling chief.

What transpired in the melee to follow will never be known exactly, pieced together as it was from the few eyewitness accounts and later secondhand reports. One thing is certain: Cook was set upon repeatedly, stabbed apparently with an iron dagger—an item of ship's trade—in a killing that was as much ritual and mythical as it was of the moment. The body of Cook/Lono, having been thus sacrificed to Kū in the name of the ruling chief, was not recovered by the British (the Lono priests later returned only a portion of the flesh to the ships at night). Cook's body was defleshed, and the bones carefully wrapped in a sennit *kāʻai* or casket in the manner accorded chiefs of the highest rank. By some Hawaiian accounts, this *kāʻai* containing Cook's remains was ritually carried on the annual *makahiki* circuit of the island for several years following.

Today the village site of Kaʻawaloa lies under a dense tangle of *koa haole* and *kiawe* trees, but the stone walls and platforms of the ancient habitations are visible from the narrow dirt road that descends from the uplands. At the shore, supposedly near the spot where he fell, is a large white obelisk, erected by Cook's countrymen in his honor. The stark contrast between the gleaming white monument and the rank, exotic vegetation smothering the rock walls offers a poetic but sorrowful visual comment on the "fatal impact" between Hawaiian civilization and the western world.

Note: The unpaved track descending from Captain Cook to Kaʻawaloa should not be attempted except in a four-wheel drive vehicle. Those opting to hike the approximately four-mile round-trip should take plenty of water, especially for the strenuous uphill return.

References: Sahlins (1981; 1985).

46. PUʻUHONUA O HŌNAUNAU

A few miles south of Kealakekua Bay lies the site of Hōnaunau, not only one of the largest, most architecturally complex and thoroughly investigated archaeological sites in the Hawaiian Islands, but also—from the native Hawaiian perspective—one of the most sacred. Situated on a natural shelf of pahoehoe lava extending into the sea, Hōnaunau was at once both a *puʻuhonua* or place of refuge, and the location of several prominent *heiau*. These *heiau* included ʻĀleʻaleʻa, a massive rectangular stone platform, and Hale o Keawe, a sacrosanct sepulchral temple that housed the remains of the Hawaiʻi Island ruling chiefs descended from ʻUmi and Līloa. Protected since 1957 as a national historical park, Puʻuhonua o Hōnaunau has been extensively restored by the National Park Service.

In traditional Hawaiian society, the behavior of individuals was highly structured according to hereditary rank, status, gender, and other attributes, and regulated by a complex system of rules, sanctions, and prohibitions: the *kapu* system. Persons who violated a *kapu* (taboo)— for example by transgressing against the person of a chief, by partaking of certain prohibited foods, or by being defeated in war—could be put to death, and became potential sacrificial victims for offerings during the *luakini heiau* rites. In various locales around the islands, however, were located *puʻuhonua* or "places of refuge," to which *kapu* breakers could flee and seek protection. Hōnaunau was a particularly famous *puʻuhonua*.

Just when the *puʻuhonua* at Hōnaunau was first established is not clear. Kamakau reported a tradition ascribing the *puʻuhonua* to the great chief Keawe-ku-i-ke-kāʻai. After careful consideration of various oral traditions, however, Dorothy Barrère believes that the site may have been founded some generations earlier, in the time of ʻEhu-kai-malino (ca. A.D. 1475 by genealogical estimates), and was reaffirmed by the famous chief ʻUmi, who conquered and unified the entire island of Hawaiʻi. The sacred sepulcher Hale o Keawe was constructed later in time, for the chief Keawe-ʻī-kekahi-aliʻi-o-ka-moku, perhaps about A.D. 1650. By the time of Captain Cook's arrival in 1779, Hōnaunau had acquired great fame not only as a *puʻuhonua*, but also as the mausoleum of the Hawaiʻi Island ruling chiefs. Indeed, according to the journal of H.M.S. *Discovery* surgeon David Samwell, Cook was taken to Hōnaunau immediately after his installation as Lono at Hikiau Heiau (see Site 44). On the passage from Kealakekua to Hōnaunau, "a Herald went before them singing, and thousands of people prostrated themselves as they passed along and put their Hands before their Faces as if it was deem'd Vilation [*sic*] or Sacrilege to look at them" (Beaglehole 1967:1162). The sanctity of the Hale o Keawe at Hōnaunau was so great that despite the widespread destruction and desecration of *heiau* and other symbols of the old religious order in 1819, this shrine remained undisturbed for a decade

Hale o Keawe, the sepulchral temple once housing the bones of Hawaiʻi Island ruling chiefs, occupies a point of land jutting into the bay at Hōnaunau.

A view of the Hale o Keawe at Hōnaunau (Site 46) as seen by William Ellis in 1843 (after Ellis, 1827).

later. About 1828, Ka'ahumanu—regent and mother of Kamehameha II—went to Hōnaunau and had the Hale o Keawe broken up, and the chiefly remains transferred to a burial cave in the Pali Kapu o Keōua at Kealakekua (eventually these bones were moved to the Royal Mausoleum in Nu'uanu Valley, O'ahu).

Archaeologically and architecturally, the Pu'uhonua o Hōnaunau complex incorporates several main constructions. Most impressive is the Great Wall, separating the pahoehoe peninsula from the surrounding terrain, and giving the whole complex the air of a fortification. The Great Wall, which runs for a total length of one thousand feet, has an average height of twelve feet, and a base width of seventeen feet, making it the largest free-standing wall known in Hawaiian archaeology. In portions, the Great Wall was constructed using a column-and-lintel method of construction (called *pa'o*), requiring fewer stones. Just inland of the Great Wall and south of Keone'ele Cove (a landing place reserved for persons of rank) is a stone-lined brackish-water fishpond, named He-lei-pālala.

The Hale o Keawe—which until 1828 housed the bones of twenty-three ruling chiefs (and probably also those of Captain Cook after his death at Ka'awaloa)—is situated at the northern end of the Great Wall. Descriptions and drawings of this temple made by missionary William Ellis (in 1823) and by Andrew Bloxam (in 1825) enabled the National Park Service to carefully reconstruct the thatch house, wooden images, and enclosing wooden fence of this sacred structure. The Rev. Ellis pushed aside the boards covering the doorway to the thatched house in 1823, and reported seeing

> many large images, some of wood very much carved, others of red feathers, with distended mouths, large rows of sharks' teeth, and pearl-shell eyes. We also saw several bundles [*kā'ai*], apparently of human bones, carefully tied up with cinet made of cocoanut fibres, and placed in different parts of the house, together with some rich shawls and other valuable articles. (1963:112)

Within the area enclosed by the Great Wall are several other important structures, chief among them 'Āle'ale'a Heiau platform. This massive rectangular structure was archaeologically excavated by Ed Ladd of the National Park Service, who demonstrated that it had been constructed in a series of seven stages, each presumably corresponding to a rededication under successive ruling chiefs. An even larger *heiau* platform, predating 'Āle'ale'a, originally was situated seaward of the latter, but has been reduced to little more than a mound of stone rubble by successive storms and tsunami. At the southern edge of the *pu'uhonua* complex, against the inner side of the Great Wall, is a low stone platform reputed to have served as a Hale o Papa, or temple where the chiefesses could worship their female deities.

References: Bryan and Emory (1986); Kamakau (1964:17–19); Kirch (1985:161–164, figs. 143–146); Ladd (1985); Rose (1992:11–24); Soehren and Tuohy (1987); Stokes (1991:104–107, figs. 51–54).

The Great Wall surrounding the Pu'uhonua o Hōnaunau is the largest free-standing prehistoric wall in the islands.

The still waters of He-lei-pālala fishpond reflect coconut palms inland of the Pu'uhonua o Hōnaunau.

Drawings of the Hale o Keawe by early European visitors enabled an accurate reconstruction of the temple house, fence, and images by National Park Service archaeologists.

47. KA LAE (SOUTH POINT)

Holes chipped through the lava rock platform at Ka Lae served as cleats for securing canoes in the often turbulent waters offshore.

The southernmost tip of Hawai'i, in Ka'ū District, was known to the ancient Hawaiians simply as Ka Lae ("the point"). Driven by northern Pacific trade winds and currents, an angry sea lashes at the eastern shore of Ka Lae, but the point of land breaks this force of nature, leaving calm waters along the protected leeward side. The confluence of ocean currents offshore, augmented by upwelling of nutrient-laden waters, makes the seas around Ka Lae rich fishing grounds, especially for large game fish such as `ahi` and `ulua`.

Despite being windswept and suffering from a lack of fresh water, Ka Lae drew early Polynesian settlers to its shores in search of fish. In the 1950s, a Bishop Museum archaeological team headed by the late Kenneth P. Emory discovered and excavated a prehistoric fishing settlement in a low sand dune called Pu'u Ali'i ("hill of chiefs"). From the midden deposits thick with the bones of pelagic fish, the excavators recovered more than seventeen hundred fishhooks of bone and shell, carved in a variety of forms and sizes. The Pu'u Ali'i dune site may have been first occupied as early as the fourth century, A.D.; in later centuries it was used as a burial place.

The Ka Lae region is rich in archaeological sites, and was declared a national historical landmark in 1962. Two sites are readily accessible near the light tower and boat launching area: Kalalea Heiau and a group of canoe mooring holes carved in the lava rock bench. Kalalea

Heiau is a small rectangular stone enclosure measuring about forty-three by thirty-five feet, close to the light tower. Adjoining the enclosure on the west is a stone-faced terrace paved with fine gravel, on which are two upright stones. These stones bear the proper names Kānemakua (on the north) and Kūmaiea (on the south), and are male and female, respectively. Inside the *heiau* enclosure and near the north wall was another upright stone, the Kū'ula or deity of fishermen. At the time that archaeologist John F. G. Stokes mapped Kalalea Heiau in 1906, it was still in use, for offerings of fish were present within the enclosure. Kalalea Heiau is a prime example of a class of smaller *heiau* known as *ko'a*, where fishermen brought offerings and performed rituals to Kū'ula in order to assure plentiful catches.

Directly seaward of Kalalea Heiau lies a rough bench of lava, with low cliffs dropping off to the sea. In the edge of this lava bench the ancient Hawaiians carved out about eighty holes or cleats, with which they could moor their canoes. The precise function of these mooring holes is uncertain; by some accounts they were used to position the canoes offshore over the most productive fishing areas. Alternatively, they may have been used to tie up canoes close to the rocky shore.

References: Kelly (1969); Kirch (1985:158–159); Stokes (1991:115–119, figs. 57–58).

The male and female stones Kānemakua and Kūmaiea stand on the 'ili'ili-paved terrace in front of Kalalea Heiau.

48. FOOTPRINTS OF KEŌUA'S ARMY

In late 1790, Kamehameha had been deeply engaged in the early stages of his intended conquest of Maui and the other islands to the west. Living on Moloka'i at the time with his warriors, Kamehameha received the news that Keōua (the younger half-brother of Kamehameha's defeated rival Kiwala'ō) had attacked the former's home lands in Kohala, Hawai'i, forcing a return to that island. The forces of Kamehameha and Keōua met in battle at Hamakua, but neither side was victorious and both withdrew. Keōua took his men to Hilo, while Kamehameha's troops retreated to Kohala. After dividing the lands of Hilo among his warrior chiefs in the traditional manner, Keōua—accompanied by several hundred warriors and their families—set out to return to his natal lands in Ka'ū.

To reach Ka'ū from Hilo, Keōua and his party took the trail running up Kīlauea and past the great crater of Halema'uma'u, abode of the fire goddess Pele. In November 1790, while they were camped at Kīlauea, a highly unusual, violent steam eruption occurred. (Only one other steam eruption has occurred in historic times—in 1924). As described by the eminent historian Ralph Kuykendall, "Keōua and his warriors were safe in their camp, but they were filled with terror and anxious to get away. On the third day they started out, in three divisions, but had not gone far when the most terrific eruption of the whole series took place, and the middle division of the army was caught in the midst of this appalling phenomenon and the warriors and children were all killed" (1938:36). Aside from the direct toll in human lives, the devastation of

Keōua's army was taken as a signal that the powerful fire goddess had put her support behind Kamehameha. The event may have broken Keōua's resolve, for the following year he acceded to a call from Kamehameha's subchiefs to come to Kawaihae and make peace with his rival. Yet Keōua must have anticipated his fate—to be speared on the beach and his body carried up to be offered as sacrifice on the *lele* altar of Kamehameha's great war *heiau* of Pu'ukoholā (see Site 31).

Perhaps the most unusual archaeological (and geological) site in the islands lies along the trail to Maunaiki in Hawaii Volcanoes National Park, where Keōua's middle division was trapped by the hot gasses and falling ash. Due to a unique combination of atmospheric and volcanic conditions, the ash hardened as it fell around the fleeing, terrified Hawaiians, capturing the impressions of their bare feet as they ran. The ash bed, only a few inches thick, was later covered with drifting cinders. In swales where the wind has blown the cinders away, sets of footprints of Keōua's army are revealed, the gripping toes forever frozen in a hopeless effort to escape.

Note: The footprints are exceedingly fragile. The set originally preserved by the Park Service under the small shed has eroded almost beyond recognition. Fresh prints are occasionally exposed by the wind; should you be lucky enough to encounter one of these sets, please do not step on or otherwise damage these endangered historical resources.

References: Ellis (1963:174–175); Kamakau (1961:152); Kuykendall (1938:36–38).

Bare toes gripped the wet, scalding hot ash as Keōua's terrified army sought desperately to flee a violent steam eruption at Kīlauea in November 1790.

The billowy pahoehoe lava at Puʻuloa has been intensively covered with petroglyphs, including thousands of circles and small cuplike depressions.

One of many thousands of petroglyph motifs pecked into the glassy pahoehoe mounds at Puʻuloa.

49. PETROGLYPHS AT PUʻULOA

On the Puna coastal plain about one and a half miles inland, and approachable today by a trail from the Chain of Craters Road in Hawaii Volcanoes National Park (the site is well signed), lies the Puʻuloa petroglyph field. With more than fifteen thousand individual petroglyph units, this is probably the single largest rock-art site in the Hawaiian Islands. The petroglyph field, situated on a broad, arid expanse of pahoehoe with only scattered low shrubs and grasses to break the monotony of lava, lies astride the old foot trail from Kealakomo to Kalapana.

Rising up in the middle of the petroglyph field is a dome or pressure ridge of pahoehoe lava, its surface literally covered with thousands of glyphs carved into the granular surface of the rock. The name Puʻuloa means "long hill," which may refer to this pahoehoe dome, but which might also be metaphorically translated "hill of long life" (Cox with Stasack 1970:23). Information obtained from Hawaiian residents of the district early in this century indicated that Puʻuloa was famous as a place where people would bring the *piko* or umbilical cord of their offspring. The visiting parent would make a hole or small cuplike depression in the lava surface, deposit the *piko* in it, and cover the hole with a stone. This practice was believed to assure the long life of the child (Cox with Stasack 1970:23, 56). Indeed, the Puʻuloa site is unique in the massive number of such small holes or depressions, which in places nearly obscure the original lava surface.

Other motifs at Puʻuloa, especially certain designs and human figures surrounding the pahoehoe dome, may have been made to commemorate the annual circum-island circuit of the Lono priests during the *makahiki* or new year festival that included the collection of tribute from each *ahupuaʻa*. Anthropologist Martha Beckwith—renowned for her recording of Hawaiian mythology and folklore—visited Puʻuloa in 1915 in the company of Konanui, who explained that these figures were "made by men who went around the district at the time of tax collecting and camped at this sacred spot" (quoted in Cox with Stasack 1970:35).

References: Cox with Stasack (1970:23–24, 56, 87, figs. 32, 37, 80); Kirch (1985:158, 271).

50. WAHA'ULA HEIAU

The stone walls of Waha'ula Heiau were barely spared Pele's wrath as the lava stopped inches from their bases. The twisted and charred steel framework of the former National Park Visitor Center lies in the distance.

In 1983, a series of lava flows began erupting from the Kūpā'ianaha vent along the Eastern Rift Zone of Kīlauea volcano, continuing throughout the decade and into the present, destroying more than one hundred homes and laying waste to thousands of acres. Between June 20 and December 7, 1989, several of these flows approached and periodically threatened to engulf the great *luakini* temple of Waha'ula ("red mouth"). While the National Park Service's visitor center was reduced to a heap of twisted steel girders, the ancient *heiau* itself was eerily spared, as the pahoehoe lava flows inexplicably halted inches from the stone walls. To those residents of Ka'ū and Puna Districts who venerate the volcano goddess, these events could only be taken as a sign of Pele's respect for the *mana* of this great temple. Indeed, it was not the first time that Pele had spared Waha'ula from her wrath; geological research has shown that the *heiau* was similarly surrounded by a vast series of lava flows sometime between about A.D. 1200 and 1450.

The prominence of Waha'ula in Hawaiian religion and tradition derives not only from seeming invincibility to volcanic destruction, but from the history of its founding by the famous voyager-priest Pā'ao. According to the version recorded by S. M. Kamakau, Pā'ao was a priest who dwelt in "Kahiki" (specifically, Wawau and 'Ūpolu), or ancestral islands to the south. Pā'ao quarreled with his older brother Lonopele, who had accused the former's son of stealing breadfruit from his garden. After a series

of altercations that resulted in the death of both the sons of Pā'ao and Lonopele, Pā'ao sailed in search of a new land. After a hazardous voyage, Pā'ao and his people reached Puna on Hawai'i Island, where he constructed his temple, called Aha'ula (Waha'ula). Later Pā'ao went on to Kohala, where he built Mo'okini Heiau (Site 27).

Pā'ao is credited in Hawaiian *mo'olelo* or traditions with introducing the ritual complex associated with the *luakini heiau*, namely the cult of human sacrifice and worship of the god Kū. This was the cult followed assiduously by the ruling chiefs, and both Kamehameha I and his heir Liholiho are known to have performed ceremonies at Waha'ula.

Architecturally, Waha'ula actually consisted of two main rectangular enclosures, the seaward one largely destroyed and said to have been the original temple; this remnant enclosure was mostly engulfed by the 1989 lava flows, although the tops of some walls remained visible. The large inland enclosure, where *luakini* rituals were performed by Kamehameha and others, was spared by the recent lava flows. This structure, with its internal features of altar and various pavements formerly covered with thatched houses, formed the basis for a scale model of a *luakini heiau* built by John F. G. Stokes for the Bishop Museum, which can still be seen on display in the Museum's Hawaiian Hall. A smaller square enclosure just seaward of the main temple was described by Stokes as the "priest's apartments."

References: Kamakau (1991:97–100); Kirch (1985:158, 259); Masse, Carter, and Summers (1991); Stokes (1991:136–144, figs. 67–71).

The carefully stacked enclosing walls of Waha'ula Heiau include pahoehoe slabs and water-rolled basalt cobbles.

GLOSSARY OF HAWAIIAN TERMS

ahupua'a. A traditional land unit, under the control of a subchief, which generally ran from the mountains to the sea.

akua. General term for a god or deity.

ali'i. Chief or person of high rank.

'ama'ama. Mullet (*Mugil cephalus*), one of the main species of fish raised in coastal ponds.

'anu'u. Part of a typical temple superstructure, a tower, frequently enclosed in white barkcloth, into which the priest would enter to receive the god's oracle.

'auwai. An irrigation canal or ditch, usually stone lined and carefully engineered, that carried stream or spring waters to a set of irrigated pondfields for cultivating taro.

awa. Milkfish (*Chanos chanos*), one of the species commonly raised in fishponds.

hala. The screwpine or *Pandanus*, the leaves of which were used to plait mats and other objects.

hālau. A longhouse, typically used to store canoes, or for *hula* instruction.

heiau. In the broadest sense, a place of worship or where sacrifices were offered. In modern usage, the term usually refers to the stone foundations of formal temple sites.

hōlua. A sled used on grassy slopes or on specially constructed stone slides.

hula. The dance of ancient Hawai'i.

'ili'ili. Fine waterworn gravel or pebbles typically used to pave house floors.

kahuna. Priest, sorcerer, or expert in any profession.

kalo. The taro plant (*Colocasia esculenta*), the corm of which was pounded and mixed with water to produce poi, the principal starch staple of ancient Hawai'i.

Kāne. One of the major deities of ancient Hawai'i; the creator god and deity of irrigated agriculture.

kapu. Taboo, sacred, or prohibited.

kī. The ti plant (*Cordyline terminalis*), one of the ancient Hawaiian cultigens with an edible root and leaves used as wrappers for food.

Kū. One of the major deities of ancient Hawai'i; the god of war.

kuaiwi. A long, straight stone wall, usually a division between dryland garden plantings (literally, "backbone").

kū'ula. A stone image of the god of fishermen.

luakini. A class of temples or *heiau* in which certain rites dedicated to the war-god Kū were performed on behalf of the reigning paramount chief; a temple of human sacrifice.

lei. A garland or necklace, often of flowers or of feathers.

lele. A stand, constructed of wooden timbers and supported upon four posts, on which sacrificial offerings were placed within *heiau* sites.

lo'i. A pondfield or irrigated plot in which the staple taro crop was cultivated.

loko 'ia. Fishpond.

loko kuapā. A fishpond enclosed by a stone wall.

maka'āinana. Commoner; the common people of the land.

mākāhā. The sluice gate of a fishpond.

mana. Supernatural or divine power; authority.

menehune. A legendary race of small people who worked at night, and were credited with constructing many fishponds and temples, especially on the islands of Kaua'i and O'ahu.

moku. A district, island, or section.

pahupū. Cut in half; a term used to describe certain Maui warriors who were tattooed black down one half of their bodies.

pali. Cliff or precipice.

piko. Navel; umbilical cord.

pōhaku ho'ohānau. Stones upon which chiefesses rested as they gave birth, hence called birthstones.

pōhaku piko. Stones in whose crevices the umbilical cord and afterbirth were hidden away.

poi. One of the main staples of ancient Hawai'i, made by pounding the starchy corm of taro and mixing it with water.

pu'uhonua. A place of refuge or asylum.

'ulu maika. A stone disc used in the *maika* or bowling game.

BIBLIOGRAPHY

Apple, R. A.
    1965 *Hawaiian Archaeology: Trails.* Bernice P. Bishop
    Museum Special Publication 53. Honolulu.

Barrera, W., Jr.
    1971 *Anaeho'omalu: A Hawaiian Oasis.* Pacific Anthro-
    pological Records 15. Honolulu: Bishop Museum.

Barrère, D. B.
    1975 *Kamehameha in Kona: Two Documentary Studies.*
    Pacific Anthropological Records 23. Honolulu: Bishop
    Museum.

Bates, M. [A Haole]
    1854 *Sandwich Island Notes.* New York: Harper &
    Brothers.

Beaglehole, J. C. (Ed.)
    1967 *The Journals of Captain James Cook: The Voyage
    of the* Resolution *and* Discovery, *1776–1780.* 2 vols.
    Cambridge: Cambridge University Press for the Hakluyt
    Society.

Beckwith, M.
    1970 *Hawaiian Mythology.* Honolulu: University of
    Hawai'i Press. (Reprint of 1940 edition.)

Bennett, W. C.
    1931 *Archaeology of Kauai.* Bernice P. Bishop Museum
    Bulletin 80. Honolulu.

Bryan, E. H., Jr., and K. P. Emory (Eds.)
    1986 *The Natural and Cultural History of Hōnaunau,
    Kona, Hawai'i.* Departmental Report 86-2. Honolulu:
    Department of Anthropology, Bishop Museum.

Buck, P. H.
    1957 *Arts and Crafts of Hawaii.* Honolulu: Bishop
    Museum Press.

Cordy, R. H.
    1970 *Pi'ilanihale Heiau Project: Phase I Site Report.*
    Departmental Report 70-9. Honolulu: Department of
    Anthropology, Bishop Museum.

    1981 *A Study of Prehistoric Social Change: The Develop-
    ment of Complex Societies in the Hawaiian Islands.* New
    York: Academic Press.

Cordy, R., J. Tainter, R. Renger, and R. Hitchcock
1991 *An Ahupua'a Study: The 1971 Archaeological Work at Kaloko Ahupua'a, North Kona, Hawai'i.* U.S. Department of the Interior, National Park Service, Western Archaeological and Conservation Center, Publications in Anthropology No. 58. (Place of publication not given.)

Cox, J. H., and E. Stasack
1970 *Hawaiian Petroglyphs.* Bernice P. Bishop Museum Special Publication No. 60. Honolulu.

Daws, G.
1973 *Holy Man: Father Damien of Molokai.* New York: Harper & Row.

Dening, G.
1988 *History's Anthropology: The Death of William Gooch.* New York: University Press of America.

Dunmore, John (Ed.)
1994 *The Journal of Jean-François de Galaup de la Pérouse, 1785–1788.* Volume I. Hakluyt Society, Second Series, Volume 179. London: The Hakluyt Society.

Earle, T. K.
1978 *Economic and Social Organization of a Complex Chiefdom: The Halele'a District, Kaua'i, Hawai'i.* Anthropological Papers of the Museum of Anthropology No. 63. Ann Arbor: University of Michigan.

Ellis, William
1842 *Polynesian Researches.* Vol. 4, *Hawaii.* London. (Reprinted by Charles Tuttle, Rutland, VT, 1969).

1963 *Journal of William Ellis. Narrative of a Tour of Hawaii, or Owhyhee . . . .* Honolulu: Honolulu Advertiser. (Originally published in 1917.)

Emerson, N. B.
1915 *Pele and Hiiaka: A Myth from Hawaii.* Honolulu: Honolulu Star-Bulletin.

Emory, K. P.
1924 *The Island of Lanai: A Survey of Native Culture.* Bernice P. Bishop Museum Bulletin 12. Honolulu.

Emory, K. P., P. C. McCoy, and D. B. Barrère
1971 *Archaeological Survey: Kahalu'u and Keauhou, North Kona, Hawaii.* Departmental Report 71-4. Honolulu: Department of Anthropology, Bishop Museum.

Emory, K. P., W. J. Bonk, and Y. H. Sinoto
1959 *Hawaiian Archaeology: Fishhooks.* Bernice P. Bishop Museum Special Publication No. 47. Honolulu.

Emory, K. P., and Y. H. Sinoto
1961 *Hawaiian Archaeology: O'ahu Excavations.* Bernice P. Bishop Museum Special Publication No. 49. Honolulu.

1969 *Age of Sites in the South Point Area, Ka'u, Hawaii.* Pacific Anthropological Records 8. Honolulu: Bishop Museum.

Emory, K. P., and L. J. Soehren
1971 *Archaeological and Historical Survey: Honokohau Area, North Kona, Hawaii.* Departmental Report 61-1 (revised edition). Honolulu: Department of Anthropology, Bishop Museum.

Fowke, G.
1922 *Archaeological Investigations. V. Archaeological Work in Hawaii.* Smithsonian Institution, Bureau of American Ethnology Bulletin 76:178–195. Washington: Government Printing Office.

Gassner, J. S. (Trans.)
1969 *Voyages and Adventures of La Pérouse. From the Fourteenth Edition of the F. Valentin Abridgment (Tours, 1875).* Honolulu: University of Hawai'i Press.

Green, R. C.
1980 *Makaha Before 1880 A.D.* Pacific Anthropological Records 31. Honolulu: Bishop Museum.

Handy, E. S. C.
1940 *The Hawaiian Planter, Volume I: His Plants, Methods and Areas of Cultivation.* Bernice P. Bishop Museum Bulletin 161. Honolulu.

Handy, E. S. C., and E. G. Handy
1972 *Native Planters in Old Hawai'i: Their Life, Lore, and Environment.* Bernice P. Bishop Museum Bulletin 233. Honolulu.

Handy, E. S. C., and M. K. Pukui
1958 *The Polynesian Family System in Ka-'u, Hawai'i.* Wellington, N.Z.: The Polynesian Society.

Handy, E. S. C., M. K. Pukui, and K. Livermore
1934 *Outline of Hawaiian Physical Therapeutics.* Bernice P. Bishop Museum Bulletin 126. Honolulu.

'I'i, J. P.
1959 *Fragments of Hawaiian History.* Honolulu: Bishop Museum Press.

Judd, L. F.
1928 *Honolulu: Sketches of the Life Social, Political, and Religious in the Hawaiian Islands from 1828 to 1861.* Honolulu: Honolulu Star-Bulletin.

Kamakau, S. M.
1961 *Ruling Chiefs of Hawaii.* Honolulu: Kamehameha Schools Press.

1964 *Ka Po'e Kahiko: The People of Old.* Honolulu: Bishop Museum Press.

1976 *The Works of the People of Old: Na Hana a ka Po'e Kahiko.* Honolulu: Bishop Museum Press.

1991 *Tales and Traditions of the People of Old: Nā Mo'olelo a ka Po'e Kahiko.* Honolulu: Bishop Museum Press.

Kelly, M.
1969 *Historical Background of the South Point Area, Ka'u, Hawaii.* Pacific Anthropological Records 6. Honolulu: Bishop Museum Press.

1971 *Kekaha: 'Aina Malo'o*. Departmental Report 71-2. Honolulu: Department of Anthropology, Bishop Museum.

1975 *Loko i'a o He'eia: He'eia Fishpond*. Departmental Report 75-2. Honolulu: Department of Anthropology, Bishop Museum.

1983 *Na Mala o Kona: Gardens of Kona*. Departmental Report 83-2. Honolulu: Department of Anthropology, Bishop Museum.

1984 *Pele and Hi'iaka Visit the Sites at Ke'e, Ha'ena, Island of Kaua'i*. Bishop Museum Publications in Education 1. Honolulu: Bishop Museum Press.

Kikuchi, W. K.
1976 "Prehistoric Hawaiian Fishponds." *Science* 193: 295–299.

Kirch, P. V.
1979 *Marine Exploitation in Prehistoric Hawai'i: Archaeological Excavations at Kalahuipua'a, Hawai'i Island*. Pacific Anthropological Records 29. Honolulu: Bishop Museum.

1984 *The Evolution of the Polynesian Chiefdoms*. Cambridge: Cambridge University Press.

1985 *Feathered Gods and Fishhooks: An Introduction to Hawaiian Archaeology and Prehistory*. Honolulu: University of Hawai'i Press.

Kirch, P. V., and M. Kelly (Eds.)
1975 *Prehistory and Ecology in a Windward Hawaiian Valley: Halawa Valley, Moloka'i*. Pacific Anthropological Records 24. Honolulu: Bishop Museum.

Kirch, P. V., and M. Sahlins
1992 *Anahulu: The Anthropology of History in the Kingdom of Hawaii*. Vol. I, *Historical Ethnography*. Vol. II, *The Archaeology of History*. Chicago: University of Chicago Press.

Kolb, M. J.
1991 *Social Power, Chiefly Authority, and Ceremonial Architecture in an Island Polity, Maui, Hawaii*. Unpublished Ph.D. dissertation, University of California, Los Angeles.

Kuykendall, R. S.
1938 *The Hawaiian Kingdom: Volume I, 1778–1854, Foundation and Transformation*. Honolulu: University of Hawai'i Press.

Ladd, E. J.
1985 *Hale-o-Keawe Archaeological Report: Archaeology at Pu'uhonua o Honaunau National Historical Park*. Western Archaeological and Conservation Center, Publications in Anthropology No. 33. National Park Service, U. S. Department of the Interior.

Ladd, E. J. (Ed.)
1973 *Makaha Valley Historical Project: Interim Report No. 4*. Pacific Anthropological Records 19. Honolulu: Bishop Museum.

Linnekin, J.
1985 *Children of the Land: Exchange and Status in a Hawaiian Community*. New Brunswick (N. J.): Rutgers University Press.

Malo, D.
1951 *Hawaiian Antiquities*. Bernice P. Bishop Museum Special Publication No. 2. Honolulu.

Masse, W. B., L. A. Carter, and G. F. Summers
1991 "Waha'ula Heiau: The Regional and Symbolic Context of Hawai'i Island's 'Red Mouth' Temple." *Asian Perspectives* 30:19–56.

McAllister, J. G.
1933 *Archaeology of Oahu*. Bernice P. Bishop Museum Bulletin 104. Honolulu.

McCoy, P. C.
1972 *Archaeological Research at Fort Elizabeth, Waimea, Kauai, Hawaiian Islands. Phase I*. Departmental Report 72-7. Honolulu: Department of Anthropology, Bishop Museum.

Menzies, A.
1920 *Hawaii Nei 128 Years Ago*. Honolulu: W. F. Wilson.

Newman, T. S.
1970 *Hawaiian Fishing and Farming on the Island of Hawaii, A.D. 1778*. Honolulu: Division of State Parks, Department of Land and Natural Resources, State of Hawaii.

Pearson, R. J.
1970 *The Archaeology of Hana: Preliminary Survey of Waianapanapa State Park*. Hawaii State Archaeological Journal 70-2. Honolulu: Department of Land and Natural Resources (State of Hawaii).

Pearson, R. J. (Ed.)
1968 *Excavations at Lapakahi: Selected Papers*. Hawaii State Archaeological Journal 69-2. Honolulu: Department of Land and Natural Resources (State of Hawaii).

1969 *Archaeology on the Island of Hawaii*. Asian and Pacific Archaeology Series No. 3. Honolulu: Social Science Research Institute, University of Hawai'i.

Pierce, R. A.
1965 *Russia's Hawaiian Adventure, 1815–1817*. Berkeley and Los Angeles: University of California Press.

Pukui, M. K.
1983 *'Olelo No'eau: Hawaiian Proverbs and Poetical Sayings*. Bernice P. Bishop Museum Special Publication No. 71. Honolulu: Bishop Museum.

Pukui, M. K., S. H. Elbert, and E. T. Mookini
1974 *Place Names of Hawaii*. (Revised and enlarged edition.) Honolulu: University of Hawai'i Press.

Rose, R. G.

1992 *Reconciling the Past: Two Basketry Kāʻai and the Legendary Liloa and Lonoikamakahiki.* Bishop Museum Bulletin in Anthropology 5. Honolulu: Bishop Museum Press.

Rosendahl, P. H.

1994 "Aboriginal Hawaiian Structural Remains and Settlement Patterns in the Upland Agricultural Zone at Lapakahi, Island of Hawaiʻi." *Hawaiian Archaeology* 3:14–70.

Rosendahl, P. H., and L. A. Carter

1988 *Excavations at John Young's Homestead, Kawaihae, Hawaii: Archeology at Puʻukoholā National Historic Site.* U. S. Department of the Interior, National Park Service, Western Archaeological and Conservation Center, Publications in Anthropology No. 47. [Place of publication not given.]

Sahlins, M.

1981 *Historical Metaphors and Mythical Realities: Structure in the Early History of the Sandwich Islands Kingdom.* Ann Arbor: University of Michigan Press.

Schilt, A. R.

1984 *Subsistence and Conflict in Kona, Hawaiʻi: An Archaeological Study of the Kuakini Highway Realignment Corridor.* Departmental Report 84-1. Honolulu: Department of Anthropology, Bishop Museum.

Soehren, L. J., and D. P. Tuohy

1987 *Archaeological Excavations at Puʻuhonua o Hōnaunau National Historical Park, Hōnaunau, Kona, Hawaiʻi.* Departmental Report 87-2. Honolulu: Department of Anthropology, Bishop Museum.

Sterling, E. P., and C. C. Summers

1978 *Sites of Oahu.* Honolulu: Bishop Museum Press.

Stokes, J. F. G.

1991 Heiau *of the Island of Hawaiʻi: A Historic Survey of Native Hawaiian Temple Sites.* Edited and Introduced by Tom Dye. Bishop Museum Bulletin in Anthropology 2. Honolulu: Bishop Museum Press.

Summers, C. C.

1964 *Hawaiian Archaeology: Fishponds.* Bernice P. Bishop Museum Special Publication No. 52. Honolulu: Bishop Museum.

1971 *Molokai: A Site Survey.* Pacific Anthropological Records 14. Honolulu: Bishop Museum.

Thrum, T. G.

1906 "Heiau and Heiau Sites Throughout the Hawaiian Islands." *The Hawaiian Annual for 1907:* 36–48.

1923 "Heiaus of Hawaii Nei." *Hawaiian Historical Society Annual Report.* Honolulu.

Tuggle, H. D.

1979 "Hawaii." In J. Jennings, ed., *The Prehistory of Polynesia,* pp. 167–199. Cambridge: Harvard University Press.

Tuggle, H. D., and P. B. Griffin (Eds.)

1973 *Lapakahi, Hawaii: Archaeological Studies.* Asian and Pacific Archaeology Series No. 5. Honolulu: Social Science Research Institute, University of Hawaiʻi.

INDEX

Thrum, Thomas G., 32, 37, 100
trails, 30, 69, 71, **87**, 91, **93**, 117

Ulaula Cave, 59
'ulu maika, 5
Ulupō Heiau, 32, **33**
'Umi-a-Līloa, 77, 109
University of California, Berkeley, 25
University of Hawai'i, 8, 45, 81, 83
upright stones, 16, **41**, 48, **68**, 69, 72, **74**, **113**

Vancouver, Captain George, 37, 102
volcanic eruptions, 114, 119
voyaging, Polynesian, 2–3, 119

Wa'awa'a Point, 91
Waha'ula Heiau, **118**, 119
Waialua, 35, 37
Wai'anae, 29, 38
Wai'ānapanapa, 71
Waiehu, 63, 67
Waihe'e, 63, 67
Waihu'ehu'e, 48
Waikīkī, 29
Waikolu, 43
Wailau, 43
Wailua (Kaua'i), 15, 16–19
Wailua Historical District, 18
Wailuku, 63, 67
Waimānalo, 4, 29
Waimea (Kaua'i), 15, 22
Waimea (O'ahu), 37
Waipi'o Valley, 106
Walker, Winslow, 7
warfare, 30, 67, 69, 70, 80, 84
war temples. See *heiau, luakini* type
Webber, John, 16, **104**, 105
wells, 58, 69, 75, 99

yams, 4
Young, John, 86